volume VII
One Show Interactive
Advertising's Best Interactive and New Media

President	David Baldwin
Executive Director	Mary Warlick
Interactive Director/Editor	Kevin Swanepoel
Associate Editor	Maiko Shiratori
Contributing Editors	Yash Egami Steve Marchese
Designer	Joy Robles
Cover/Divider Page Design & Photo Credits	Goodby, Silverstein & Partners
DVD Production	AVA Book Production Pte. Ltd. Email: production@avabooks.com.sg
Published by	One Club Publishing LLC 21 E. 26th Street, 5th Floor New York, NY 10010 Tel: +1.212.979.1900 Fax: +1.212.979.5006 Email: publishing@oneclub.org Web: www.oneclub.org In Association with The One Club
Distribution (USA and Canada)	Rockport Publishers 3 Commercial Street Gloucester, MA 01930, USA Web: www.rockpub.com
Distribution (International)	AVA Distribution Tel: +41.78.600.5109 Email: sales@avabooks.ch Web: www.avabooks.ch
First Printing	ISBN: 8-929837-24-X
Production and Separation	AVA Book Production Pte. Ltd.
Sponsors	DoubleClick Media Temple Yahoo!
Image Partner	Getty Images

contents

THE ONE CLUB

The one club

Based in New York City, The One Club was founded in 1975 and is a non-profit organization dedicated to maintaining the highest standards of creativity in advertising. Its 1,000 members include many of advertising's most respected art directors and copywriters, as well as students of advertising.

Mission

As part of its mission to promote high standards of creative excellence, The One Club produces the advertising industry's most prestigious awards program, The One Show. Judged by a panel of the advertising industry's elite creative directors, this annual event acknowledges excellence in art direction, design, and copywriting in a variety of categories, including television, radio, newspapers, magazines, billboards and public service. The coveted One Show "Gold Pencils" are regarded as the zenith of achievement in the advertising world.

In 1998, The One Club launched One Show Interactive, the first awards show dedicated exclusively to advertising in new media. With the One Show Interactive awards, The One Club extended its mission of recognizing creative excellence to the new media field.

Now in its sixth year, One Show Interactive is recognized as the most prestigious competition for advertising in new media.

Programs

The One Club regularly produces a variety of events and programs that encourage aspiring advertising professionals to hone their craft.
These programs include:

- "Gold on Gold" Lectures (award-winning industry professionals discussing the creative process)

- Portfolio Reviews

- The One Show College Competition

- Creative Workshops

- one. a magazine – a quarterly publication by and for advertising creatives

- One Club Gallery Exhibitions

- The One Show Annual, the indispensable hard cover reference showcasing the best advertising worldwide

- One Show Interactive Annual, the first book of its kind, highlighting the best new media advertising

Education

n 1995, The One Club established an education department, dedicated to fostering the creative talents of advertising students nationwide. The department sponsors educational programs and events, and administers scholarships to outstanding students in advertising programs at a select number of colleges and advertising schools throughout the country.

david baldwin
President, The One Club

What does 'interactive' even mean anymore? Let me explain.

A long time ago, the industry was populated with print experts. They churned out beautiful, well-written print ads.

Then along came this new medium called television. The agencies were in a quandary. Should they create a new department that did television separately, or should they teach their old dogs some new tricks and have everyone do everything? We all know the answer to that question.

And yet we find ourselves in such a place again now. The truth is, interactive work is becoming so much a part of the mainstream that it's almost a little silly to talk about it on its own. More often than not the interactive work (Is that term even big enough anymore?) is the pointy part of the stick rather than the handle.

Many clients don't even bother with mainstream general advertising anymore. Or instead they use their advertising for the sole purpose of getting you to a computer to spend some time with their brand.

Some of the interactive companies are starting to do advertising. The ad agencies are doing terrific interactive work. Design firms are doing all of it. The line has officially blurred, ladies and gentlemen. And it's produced one heck of a show.

Spend a little time with this book and you'll be rewarded with some terrific, smart work that will sometimes make you laugh, sometimes make you think, and often make you ask, "How the heck did they do that?"

kevin swanepoel
Interactive Director, The One Club

This is the eighth year that One Show Interactive has been setting standards for creative excellence in interactive advertising for the new media industries.

One Show Interactive Volume VII has been expanded to include outlines from the creative teams that worked on the work to give you a better understanding of the brief and the objectives and how they achieved them.

It's clear now that Fallon's "BMW Films" campaign, launched in 2001, has created a whole new genre of interactive advertising. It's becoming increasingly familiar to hear about clients putting engaging content online—whether it be in the form of short films, interactive games or by allowing consumers to create their own music mixes and re-mixes from such high profile artists as David Bowie. In each instance, brands are enjoying the benefits of retaining consumer interest and exposure for prolonged periods of time. Clients are constantly looking for new approaches in marketing their brands by break away from the traditional 30-second TV commercial. They are exploring the Internet, trying to find ways that they can immerse the consumer in their brand.

For years games have lived online, but recently clients have begun to actively explore the genre. That's why One Show Interactive introduced a new category this year for innovative work in the area of brand gaming. The response was fantastic—we received many well-targeted entries that ranged from simple kids' games to high-end online games for the fanatic.

I applaud the thirty international interactive judges from fifteen countries who spent literally hundreds of hours judging the entries this year, and on behalf of The One Club I thank them for their effort, their insight and their dedication to honoring the best interactive work our industry has to offer.

Matt Freeman
One Show Interactive Jury Chairman
Chief Executive Officer
Tribal DDB, New York

Well, amidst the detritus of war, global terrorism, SARS, the "jobless recovery," and Janet Jackson's unsheathed mammary, Interactive emerged from the ashes this past year—and it emerged stronger than ever.

Teens and young adults in the US now spend more time online than with any other medium—even more than TV. Over 70 percent of Americans are now online. Nearly 40 percent have broadband.

This strange, exciting, complex, melodramatic "new medium" is now officially a Mass Medium—a corporately sanctioned member of the marketing club. It is now legitimate.

So is the adventure over? Did getting big mean we got boring?
Judging by the entries this year, the answer is a resounding "No."

Along with huge growth in online investments came huge growth in online thinking. Bigger ideas. Better execution. And some of the most fresh and inventive work to be found in any medium.

From São Paulo to Sydney—for big brands and local stores alike, the interactive work we judged all seemed to take a great global leap forward this year. It made the judging (well, at least the final judging) more of an honor than a chore.

So, a sincere thanks to all the judges. And here's to the New Mass Medium...

Interactive Judges

interactive judges

Mauro Alencar
Blast Radius, Vancouver

Suzana Apelbaum
AgênciaClick, São Paulo

Sam Ball
Lean Mean Fighting Machine,
London

Juan Luis Bastos
Zentropy, Madrid

Jeff Benjamin
Crispin Porter + Bogusky, Miami

Joakim Borgström
DoubleYou, Barcelona

Keith Butters
The Barbarian Group, Boston

Warren Corbitt
one9ine, New York

Dirk Eschenbacher
OgilvyOne worldwide, Beijing

Kevin Farnham
Method, San Francisco

Lorenzo Formenti
Noparki, Milano

Ze Frank
zefrank.com, Brooklyn

Toshiya Fukuda
777interactive, Tokyo

Dominic Goldman
OgilvyOne worldwide, Singapore

Bob Greenberg
R/GA, New York

Angel Herraiz
Herraiz Soto & Co., Barcelona

Andy Hobsbawm
AGENCY.COM, London

Ashadi Hopper
channel:one, Sydney

Katerina Martchouk
Periscope, Minneapolis

Will McGinness
Goodby, Silverstein & Partners,
San Francisco

Arnaud Mercier
elixirstudio, Marseille

Sascha Merg
Sas21.de, Hamburg

Brian Merrifield
Saatchi & Saatchi, Wellington

Nils Petter Nordskar
Virtual Garden, Oslo

Ted Persson
Great Works, Stockholm

Todd Purgason
Juxt Interactive, Newport Beach

Vivian Rosenthal
Tronic Studio, New York

Sebastian Royce
Glue, London

Hirozumi Takakusaki
Dentsu, Tokyo

Marco Tinelli
Full Six, Lavallois-Perre

Mauro Alencar
Blast Radius, Vancouver

Judge's choice: 404
Client: AgênciaClick
ID: 04222N

Although specific piece didn't win a pencil, I think it deserves to be mentioned due to its unconventional approach to corporate self-promotional messaging and production quality.

It is a well-produced, tightly-designed Flash experience that makes good use of interactive video, text and sound to show how details we sometimes take for granted or underestimate when developing Internet work can eventually jeopardize entire projects and, in some cases, leave nasty stains on the client's brand.

I loved how they used humor to talk about topics like scope and risk management. The cinematic visual treatment, with thriller-movies-style, black-and-white graphics, along with the SUPERB soundtrack gave this piece a truly dramatic feel that we barely see every day on the Web. To sum up: great idea, great design, great video and audio production, great Flash work.

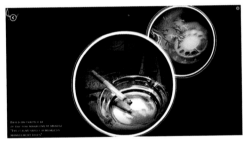

Suzana Apelbaum
AgênciaClick, São Paulo

Judge's choice: ASICS Marathon
Client: ASICS Deutschland
ID: 04145N

After Flash was incorporated as a basic tool to make good animations, few works managed to distinguish themselves using only text and HTML. Virtual Marathon is an example of the strength of a good creative concept, that even working with simple technology succeeds in assuring an enormous visual and sensorial impact.

During the interaction, the play makes one feel each one of the sensations experienced during a dispute such as a marathon—from the will to be the winner, through the concern with the adversaries and fatigue, until the point of physical exhaustion when it is no longer possible to keep pressing scroll to arrive at the final line. This is, indeed, living a brand experience. This is one of the biggest jewels that the Web can offer to the advertising market.

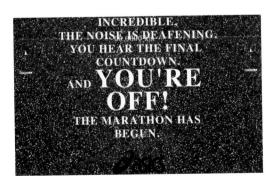

Judges' choice NEC ecotonoha project
client NEC Corporation
ID 04025N

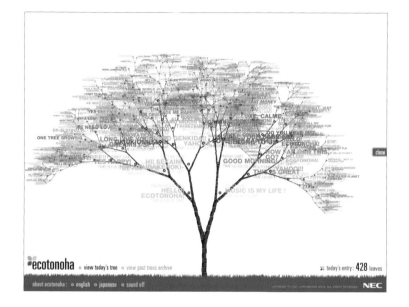

a › Sam Ball

b › Juan Luis Bastos

c › Nils Petter Nordskar

d › Todd Purgason

Sam Ball
Lean Mean Fighting Machine, London

My favorite entry to this year's One Show was the NEC ectonoha project. This site encourages people to write a message that will represent a leaf on a virtual tree; in return NEC will plant a real tree after a certain amount of messages have been submitted.

The work is executed with a charm and subtlety rarely seen online. The process of creating your leaf is simple and intuitive and, above all, is an enjoyable experience.

The work is not selling a specific product, but it is one of the best pieces of online branding I have seen. Many big corporations strive to look echo-friendly and have failed; in this instance they have pulled it off.

Juan Luis Bastos
Zentropy, Madrid

It has a deep concept and interactivity that goes beyond the media itself. It improves the environment through people's participation and collaboration. Moreover, the brand assumes a second role to let the users be the main characters. All this with a clean, strong and simple execution. I could be fascinated for days and days, enjoying, without navigating anywhere else.

Nils Petter Nordskar
Virtual Garden, Oslo

At the very end of my jury work, before the results from all over the world came in, I asked one of my colleagues at Virtual Garden to take a look at a couple of jobs that I felt really stood out from the rest. One was Volvo's Inside Story campaign, and the other was the NEC ecotonoha project. Living in Oslo, Norway, it felt good to see that Scandinavian online marketing is at a top level internationally. When we studied the thoughts and the creativity in the NEC ecotonoha project, there really wasn't any doubt about which job I loved the most. This is simply irresistible Web creativity—one cannot possibly not like it. It stands out as a concept and in the way it was so excellently executed. When the rest of the juries' points came in, it seemed I was showing my colleague a real winner.

Todd Purgason
Juxt Interactive, Newport Beach

I would say that for my Judge's Choice, I would have to pick NEC's ecotonoha project. It may be a response to seeing something that uses interactive to promote a brand that gives rather than takes as we are so often doing in all mediums of advertising. But I also would have to say that it is very rare to see a project bridge between communication, concept, culture and action in a way that is so sublimely simple and yet so affectingly functional. When you create a leaf on a tree you instantly feel a part of something bigger than yourself, something bigger than technology, something even bigger than adding a new life to the planet. You feel more human as if this technology were a bridge of humanity that connects you with other humans who all desire to see the world become a better place. It is also quite inspiring to see a brand step out and do something so unique, both in the concept of the project as well as the concept of the interactive vehicle, that makes it happen. It makes me wonder what kind of impact could be made if we all started applying just a bit of creative thinking and a bit of financial resources to the countless other issues our world faces.

⊐eff Benjamin
Crispin Porter + Bogusky, Miami

⊐udge's choice: Beta-7
client: ESPN Videogames/Sega
ID: 04042N

I was prejudging the One Show when out of nowhere some loon came running over and crashed into me. He said his name was Beta-7. I've been in the hospital ever since.

I just know Sega had something to do with this, even though I can't prove anything. I'm still trying to get more info out of the police, but it's like pulling teeth. I'll keep you posted when I hear anything else.

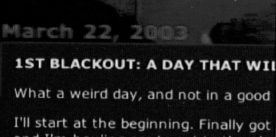

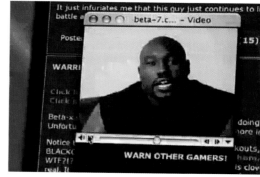

vivian rosenthal
Tronic Studio, New York

judge's choice: The Mystery of Dalarö
client: Volvo Car Corporation
ID: 04043N

judge's choice: Beta-7
client: ESPN Videogames/Sega
ID: 04042N

The new trend of integrated marketing, while clearly being embraced by the ad world, needs to be approached differently than traditional ads. With the correct approach that is sensitive to each of the various mediums, the results are noteworthy and unique, as evidenced in Beta-7 and The Mystery of Dalarö. On the other hand, integrated marketing runs the risk of blindly transferring one technique that is successful in one medium onto another, yielding uninteresting, confusing or irrelevant results. Beta-7 and Dalarö stand out as examples for the future of integrated marketing. They are both experiential and intriguing. The viewer is made to feel that he is on a journey of discovery through a narrative, thereby seemingly decreasing the focus on the brand or product. In this reversal, the viewer actually becomes more interested in the brand since he spends more time on the ad. Hopefully we will continue to see such dynamic and provocative work as Beta-7 and The Mystery of Dalarö in the coming year.

Judges' choice Vodafone Future Vision
client Vodafone Group Services
id 04026N

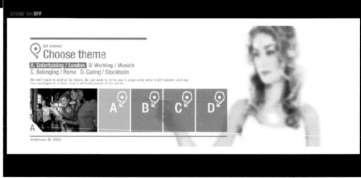

Joakim Borgström
DoubleYou, Barcelona

Also Chose:
Judge's choice: Acura 2004 TL Exterior Showroom
client: American Honda Motor Company
ID: 04138N

a > Joakim Borgström

b > Bob Greenberg

c > Andy Hobsbawm

d > Ashadi Hopper

Has anyone ever stopped to think how long it takes to visualize almost 600 projects? Let's do a simple calculation: 600 x 4 min (it's the average time I feel it's taken me to visit every piece, counting only the actual time from clicking until closing the window).

Maybe it's not that impressive, but I can assure you that it has been a really interesting experience. Forty real hours surfing! Wow. It has been really pleasing and I think I now have a good grasp of the current state of affairs of world-wide creativity.

Personally, I feel advertising pieces can be divided into two categories: those that try to find a clear creative concept consistent with the brand, and those that try to seduce you with its production side. Maybe the latter is exactly what has surprised me—huge productions made specifically for the Web.

There are two projects that I would highlight. One of them is the Vodafone Future Vision and the second is the showroom for the Acura TL. Both of them use voice-over as one of its main elements. I really like not having to read—we all know that almost nobody reads text on the Web. Thus, entering a site and simply being guided by voice is fantastic. Both sites have also taken a good care of the loading and the small details, small transitions and visual effects. Chapeau!

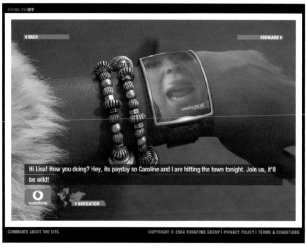

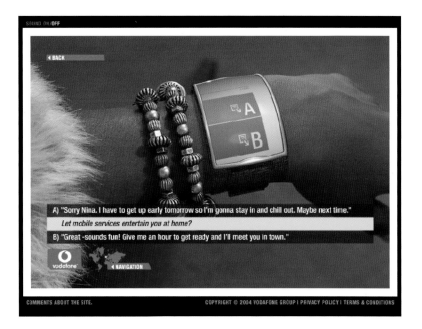

Bob Greenberg
R/GA, New York

As a judge for the 2004 One Show Interactive, I was very impressed with the Vodafone Future Vision B2C Web site.

I remember many years ago, John Sculley, the CEO of Apple, presented the "Knowledge Navigator"—Apple's view of the future. The system incorporated a silly "butler-type" guy who would solve all of your communication problems through a tricked-out Newton PDA with voice activation. What a relief that Steve Jobs eventually returned to Apple with some wonderful futuristic devices (currently incorporated into the beautifully designed Apple stores).

Many corporations such as IBM, AT&T, Silicon Graphics, etc., have tried their hand at presenting their version of the future...unsuccessfully.

But this year's Vodafone entry truly succeeded in nearly every way, from the casting, photography, set design, music, sound effects, copy, special effects, and more importantly, the future scenarios of the device themselves.

Everything worked seamlessly...congratulations to the Vodafone team!

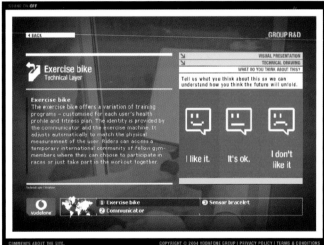

Andy Hobsbawm
AGENCY.COM, London

Just when I was beginning to think the Web had turned into the Detroit Motor Show, innovative and wonderfully clever pieces of interactivity showed up like NEC's ecotonoha project or Poke's Very Public Art Gallery and Global Rich List campaigns, which went some way to restoring my faith in the medium. (Although I have to admit, I did rather like Tribal's cool, weird, mini-universe in Discover The Phaeton—even if it was about a car). For e-commerce, I loved the brilliant Linotype Fontcomparer online application. I can't imagine the market for comparing glyphs on "DeutscheBahnAG One-Normal" with "Fairfield LT Heavy-Italic" at 500% zoom being better served. For utterly shameless self-promotion (rather marvelous that there's actually a category for this!), who can resist the Gorgeous Web site? (Some of the judges, obviously, since it only got Silver.) Finally, I particularly enjoyed Vodafone's Future Vision piece. It's a lovely blend of traditional and richly interactive storytelling. All in all, a fine example of non-linear narrative and rather inspiring—but then I've always been a sucker for that future vision stuff...

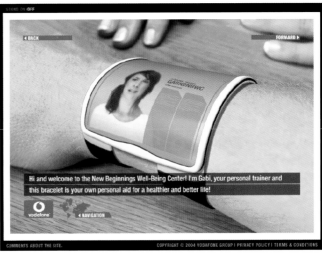

Ashadi Hopper
channel:one, Sydney

While sites such as BMW Films are regularly touted at award shows as the future for brands online, I feel that such sites have failed to capitalize on the most important aspect online: Interactivity. Content-wise, BMW Films was in a league of its own, though it was largely a linear experience after pressing play. In contrast, Vodafone's Future site goes one step further by combining a strong narrative, stunning visuals along with a style of interactivity that encourages the user to explore, rather than be lead. Each click of the mouse transports you into a futuristic scenario where you can explore the various technologies and their applications. Users are encouraged to give their feedback on Vodafone's view of the future through a well-integrated visual response survey that simply requires the user to click one of three icons. Interactivity means choice, and Vodafone delivers choice by breaking down content into a number of information layers, enabling the user to take control over their level of involvement. If you're like me, you'll choose to be emersed in the detail for an hour, clicking everything to ensure you haven't missed a thing.

judges' choice Very Public Art Gallery
client Britart.com
ID 04052N

a › Warren Corbitt
b › Dirk Eschenbacher
c › Ze Frank
d › Will McGinness

warren corbitt
oneⁿine, New York

It's funny in an age of high gloss and glam in the interactive sphere—where everything that can move should—to be writing about a campaign structured around something as mundane as a shop window and the cellular in your pocket. The Very Public Art Gallery for britart.com—where passers-by bid on art displayed in a storefront display—represents a beautiful simplification—a pure reduction—of practice, concept and technology. The 3-D rendering and navigations that "go bump in the night" pale in comparison, leaving one's memory as quickly as the screen can refresh to the next techno-derivative beat.

dirk eschenbacher
OgilvyOne worldwide, Beijing

Wireless is probably the most direct form of one-to-one communication between a brand and its consumers. After a huge hype a few years ago, this medium found its place mostly in very promotion-driven campaigns. Admittedly, it is hard to use it on a more sophisticated level as you have only a few characters to play with. I was very inspired when I saw "the world's first ever public art auction," done for britart.com. A simple idea: use wireless technology to start the communication between the gallery and the consumer, then follow up with messages to the mobile phone and direct participants to the Web site for further communication. The campaign delivers a solid interactive experience and makes it fun to spend the money. It's an excellent example of using technology in an innovative and exciting way. Bravo!

ze frank
zefrank.com, Brooklyn

I love the spirit of this piece—that it moves the appreciation and valuation of art out into the open. I like the idea of the public transaction—stopping on a street corner in front of a painting that catches my eye and immediately thinking about its relationship to me, both aesthetically and in terms of the amount I would bid. It sets up a wonderful conversation between the pedestrian and the art world outside of the sometimes oppressive and intimidating culture of the gallery. The use of tech in this project is simple, approachable and transparent. A beautiful example of a well-executed online/offline project.

will mcginness
Goodby, Silverstein & Partners, San Francisco

The NEC ecotonoha Web site was a beautiful example of what the Web can be and I'm sure it will be written about. So, my personal choice for the annual is the Britart Very Public Art Gallery. Like Beta-7, it was refreshing to see a project breaching the barriers of what we typically assume interactive work to be. I found the use of cellular technology paired with a simple concept such as the art auction to be both practical and inventive.

In addition, I was disappointed to not see the Trick-or-Treat Beat entry of the new Brand Gaming category make it to the finals. Not since the Infamous Worm Game, have I been distracted into hours of procrastination.

Keith Butters
The Barbarian Group, Boston

Judge's choice: Trick-or-Treat Beat
Client: Cartoon Network
ID: 1352

Most of the work I was impressed with (Vodafone, ecotonoha, and others) were duly awarded Pencils, but none kept me up into the wee hours of the morning like a harmless little game about trick-or-treating. This game was understandably overlooked in the Brand Gaming category, since it wasn't really advertising anything (at the time). However, I found it to be the most addictive, productivity-destroying distraction I've seen online in a long time. Since judging the One Show, I have played this game, as a brand gaming advertising experience for Dexter's Laboratory. It's unfortunate that we were not able to judge the game in that context.

A lot of brand gaming experiences on the Web seem to lose sight of the reason to make a game in the first place. So many times it's all brand and no game. Users leave as quickly as they come, and they don't tell their friends. Games need to be fun. Operation Trick-or-Treat Beat is really fun, and subsequently, successful.

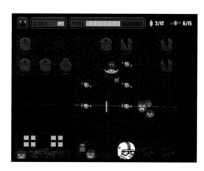

Kevin Farnham
Method, San Francisco

Judge's choice: BMW X5
Client: BMW
ID: 04013N

There are a lot of factors involved in creating a great online experience: strategy, concept, creativity, interactivity, branding, design, technology, production, client aptitude, budget, time, project management, talent—the list goes on. Occasionally, you can see where everything is in synch. For me, the BMW X5 mini-site is an example of it all coming together.

It is rare to see a site where the concept marries well to the product, the design marries well to the brand, technology is used appropriately and the experience really gels. This site invites exploration, the photography is beautiful, and the Flash work is solid. I felt that they really nailed a mood here and made someone want to learn more about the product. A well-designed, thoughtfully considered site that made me want to buy the car. Bravo.

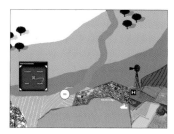

Lorenzo Formenti
Noparki, Milano

Judge's choice: Touareg
Client: Volkswagen
ID: 04132N

Simple, clear and effective. I liked the style used in the 'features' section a lot. I've spent some considerable time here while exploring, which is something I haven't done in a long time. Bravi!

Toshiya Fukuda
777interactive, Tokyo

Judge's choice: Nikeplay.com-The Game
Client: American Nike
ID: 04047N

Nike's "tag" TV commercial was wonderful.

But this "tag" online game is also wonderful.

Such a combination of ad and experiences changes the future of advertising.

 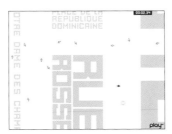

 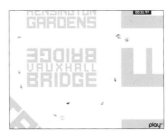 

Dominic Goldman
OgilvyOne worldwide, Singapore

Judge's choice: FootBag
Client: Coca-Cola Brasil
ID: 04068N

In the early days of interactive, our screens were cluttered with online ads that featured crude and clunky animated gifs. To make matters worse, decent ideas were nowhere in sight. The technology may have advanced, but the clutter remains. And all too often, weak interactive ideas try to hide behind slick executions. However, "FootBag" a banner for Coca-Cola Football Sponsorship, has managed to communicate a strong, simple idea with the good-old animated gif. Moreover, the concept is absolutely right for the Brazilian market—it's based on the recycle character on the side of the Coke can who controls the ball beautifully and juggles it to perfection. Sweet.

Angel Herraiz
Herraiz Soto & Co., Barcelona

Judge's choice: FootBag
Client: Coca-Cola Brasil
ID: 04068N

Judge's choice: I-Shake-U
Client: Mitsubishi Motors
ID: 04016N

I still think that the most fresh and powerful ideas come from Brazil. If you add good production to this, we find work like that of the Coca-Cola can that recycles itself with the scroll bar.

For the wealth of interactivity and the graphic and production quality, another outstanding piece for me has been the Mitsubishi's I-shake-U.

However, I was already familiar with both these pieces before the One Show.

I haven't noted any trends, surprises or huge revelations at this edition. I was a little disappointed, perhaps because we are all so well accustomed, by Nike's general work. I can still see significant resources and accomplishment behind their pieces, but I feel new and powerful ideas are lacking this time round.

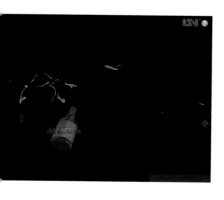

Brian Merrifield
Saatchi & Saatchi, Wellington

Judge's choice: I-Shake-U
client: Mitsubishi Motors Corporation
ID: 04016N

To me, the most memorable entry is i-shake-u.com, which is a Dentsu creation and rightly deserves a Gold.

I-Shake-U grabs the user's attention right from the get-go by using a simple act of shaking the mouse and quirky animation. This type of unique interaction emphasizes the way I-Shake-U strengthens the relationship between user and computer throughout the brand experience.

The games, which focus on the experience of driving without cars, is pure genius. Which totally adds to the unique etherealness of the experience. Mitsubishi Motors were brave to go for the concept of a car site featuring next to no cars until the end. The games are simple to play and have lots of replay value. They have a 'Dance Dance Revolution' type interaction to them that makes them familiar for those who have played 'Simon Says,' which is almost everybody.

The design is a quirky mix of slick Japanese vector graphics and distressed/punk inspired anti-media static. Which all goes brilliantly with the underlying anti-advertising message which leads you on a quest for the search and 'evolution' of your inner self. Which just happens to be a Mitsubishi Lancer Evolution.

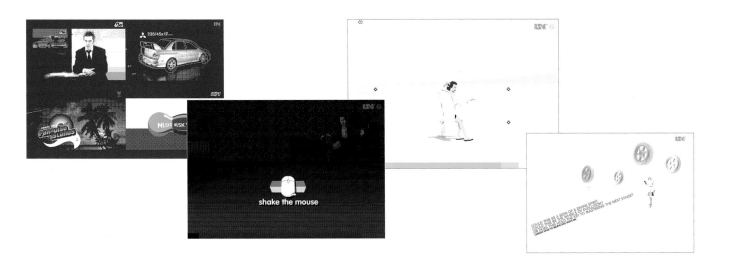

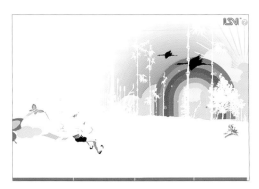

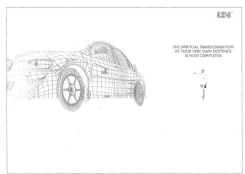

katerina martchouk
Periscope, Minneapolis

Judge's choice: Skyhigh Airlines
Client: Alaska Airlines
ID: 04045N

One of my most favorite entries was Skyhigh Airlines, an Integrated Branding campaign for Alaska Airlines. The concept is a smart kind of funny, and the campaign elements work together flawlessly. I have the deepest respect for WONGDOODY and their client who weren't afraid to push a fun idea so far—it seems to have taken on a life of its own. Well done.

arnaud mercier
elixirstudio, Marseille

Judge's choice: Nike San Silvestre Vallecana 2003
Client: American Nike
ID: 04135N

To judge this competition, I went through 450 different interactive experiences. A lot of them were very good, some were even excellent, but only one managed to leave me an indelible impression: Nike San Silvestre. I believe the success of this campaign is based on a really strong and yet simple concept that works really well online (the escaping bear).

On top of that, the final pieces (banners, Web site) are done really well—dynamic, sound driven, quality of execution, eye for details, small loading time—this is Flash used at its best, no gimmicks, just what's needed of animation and transition.

A true interactive experience. I really wished I had done this.

sascha merg
Sas21.de, Hamburg

judge's choice: Launch
client: Napster
ID: 04129N

I think I looked through 400 Web sites and banners, and I still remember it was very refreshing to see Napster's banner ad campaign. You feel how much fun the creators had to do these little animation movies! The product seems pleasant to work for, since its very rebellious history.

ted persson
Great Works, Stockholm

judge's choice: Global Rich List
client: CARE International UK
ID: 04061N

Many of the 594 (I think) entries I went through looked enormously well. But quite a few of them lacked a strong idea.

The Global Rich List stood out—the site might not be the most beautiful creation you've seen, but it really gets you thinking.

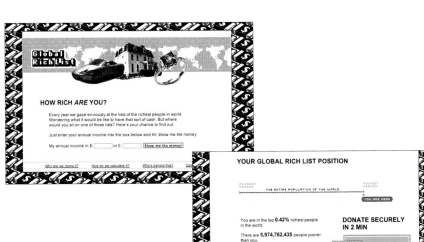
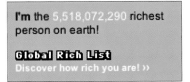

sebastian royce
Glue, London

judge's choice: Map
client: Audi
id: 04001N

My personal favorite work this year was the Audi drop down banner. Admittedly, it's not a very controversial choice as the judges awarded it a Gold in the single banner category. For me it has everything a (restricted file size) online ad should have. Fantastic design of a single and very strong visual idea, accompanied by simple yet rewarding interaction. It's a great piece of work. On a different issue, I noticed this year that there were many more audio/visual experiences right across the board. The use of sound to enhance executions is certainly on the up driven by the rapid Broadband penetration we have seen over the last twelve months. It was used to great effect in a number of pieces of work we saw and as long as it is used wisely—to improve the user experience, then long may it continue.

I think it is also worth mentioning that a lot of the best advertising didn't look like direct response stuff. Click-through wasn't the sole form of interaction required. Clients are learning that getting people to visit a site does not have to be the be-all and end-all of online advertising. Providing them with an interesting interactive experience within an ad can be more than enough.

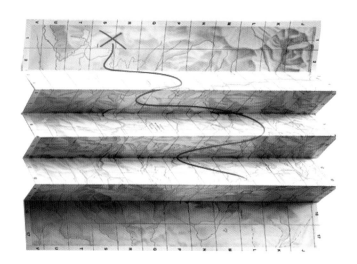

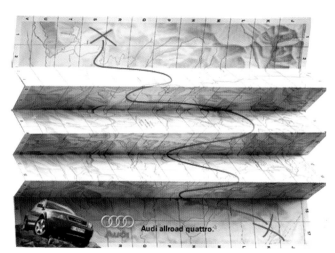

Hirozumi Takakusaki
Dentsu, Tokyo

judge's choice: Ohayo Players
client: Tanaka Garden
ID: 04207N

This simple game is based on an old Japanese children's play. Even for the first time, the visitor can play without a manual. Usually network games can be split into two groups: complicated, difficult games or too easy, uninteresting games. However, this game got valuable results—easy and interesting. As we can use a Web camera as an input device like a mouse, the original interaction system can give unique effects and impressions to visitors. Design and illustration details are also important. They have a strong impact created by the original blend of Japanese and some other Asian essences. Its character and sound design can't be forgotten.

Considering the small size of the agency, it must have been difficult to harmonize art direction, sound design and original interactive system, and to accomplish such an intricate game. This is a good example of a new interactive idea, and a great time killer.

Marco Tinelli
Full Six, Lavallois-Perre

judge's choice: Nike (various)

What struck me most is the overall outstanding quality of the entire Nike work presented. It's all there: great marketing ideas, strong customer focus, and impeccable execution.

The most impressive aspect of such overall high quality is that there are multiple agencies behind all the awarded (and non-awarded) creative.

Ad work, branding work, e-commerce work...it's a pleasure seeing how a company like Nike understands the interactive media and leverages all its fundamental assets to deliver great marketing that works.

NikeLab, Nike Id, Hooptown, The San Silvestre Vallecana... Nike delivers great value to consumers through daring ideas and impeccable execution.
An example for the entire industry!

Client of the Year

CLIENT OF THE YEAR: NIKE

Bryan Finke
Digital Marketing Director,
Nike U.S.A.

Nike is very honored to be recognized as the One Show Interactive Client of the Year for the second year in a row. On behalf of the Global Nike Digital Marketing Teams I would like to thank our interactive creative agencies (R/GA, Framfab, AKQA, Daiko Advertising, DoubleYou, The Barbarian Group, IA Collaborative and henderson bas) for their award winning contributions. The digital medium enables individuals around the world to directly interact with the Nike brand in new and unique ways. Nike is committed to maximizing these interactions-delivering inspiring and innovative brand experiences that help individual athletes improve their performance. Our work demonstrates our commitment to connect with the athlete regardless of their individual sport or activity and our continued drive to push the limits of what's possible in the medium. For us, there is no finish line.

1 › DoubleYou/Barcelona
Nike San Silvestre
Vallecana 2003
04005N

2 › R/GA/New York
Hooptown
04020N

3 › R/GA/New York
Nike Lab
04028N

4 >

5 >

6 >

7 >

8 >

9 >

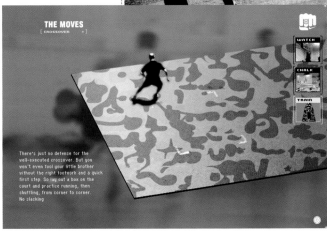

4 > R/GA/New York
Nike Goddess
04038N

5 > Framfab/Copenhagen
Nike iD
04039N

6 > Framfab/Copenhagen
Goooooal!
04046N

7 > DoubleYou/Barcelona
Nikeplay.com
04047N

8 > AKQA/San Francisco
Keep the Ball Alive
04053N

9 > AKQA/San Francisco
Is This You
04102N

The armadillo plays quietly in the meadow·.

EL OSO EXISTE.

< 17

< 18

19 >

< 28

< 21

22 >

< 23

Best of Show

A TREE GROWS ONLINE

Participation is one of the most fundamental elements of interactivity. NEC Corporation's stunning use of a community "tree" model to advertise their environmental contributions through IT technology, represents a true synthesis of new media capability and creativity. The execution and art direction perfectly capture the roots of their corporate slogan — "Empowered by Innovation."

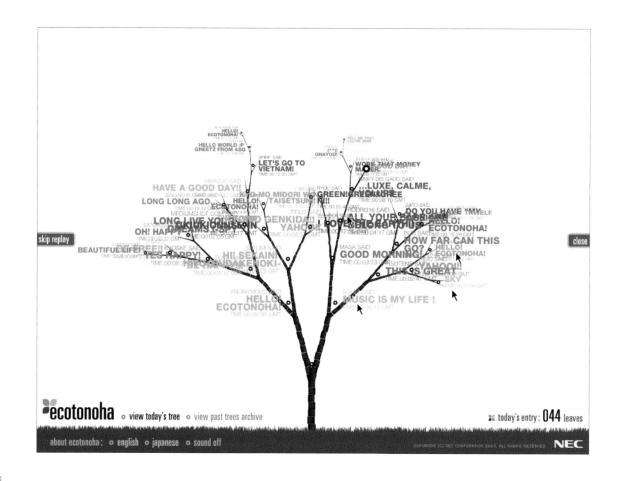

Art Director:
Yugo Nakamura
Writer:
Toru Ejima
Programmers:
Tadahiko Sato, Hitoshi Aizawa
Production Company:
NEC Media Products
Producers:
Masahiro Toki, Teruhiko Enomoto
Designers:
Ken-ichi Yamanaka, Yosuke Fukasawa
Creative Director:
Fumitake Arano
URL:
http://eco.adnec.com/eco_unlimited/
ad_en.html
ID:
04025N

Gold Award:
Corporate Image B2C—Web Sites

Given the overall amount of users, discuss some of the technical issues of the execution.
There were 60,000 entries from July to December 2003. We greatly appreciate that there were so many participants. Upon production of the site, we kept one important point in mind—that users should be able to enjoy clicking and operating the site. Further, we hoped that all participants could feel a sense of being nurtured through enjoying simple and beautiful visuals and music.

Discuss the art direction and client's brief. Was balancing the organic and technological elements difficult?

Our client is the Advertising Department of NEC Corporation. They have been executing advertising campaigns featuring a main theme of environmental contribution through IT technology. They intended to make their tree-planting activities in Australia widely known while letting people feel empathy with and perhaps surprise at this project, thereby linking this to NEC's branding efforts.

We requested art direction from Mr. Yugo Nakamura once the concept of the project was approved. His sophisticated artistic expression led to NEC's advanced image which reflects the corporate slogan "Empowered by Innovation."

While there are various ways to help the environment, we would like to conduct this specific project by letting people participate through the Internet. In order for users to feel the existence of other users more clearly, we set the number of objects that can be displayed on one screen based on the limits of Flash technology.

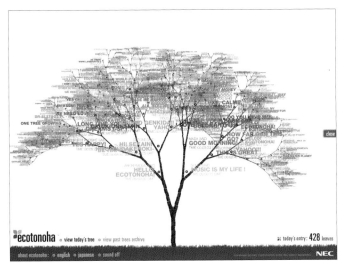

How did the users react to the piece?
How important was the aspect of community?
After the project was launched, we were surprised to see more oversea participants than we had expected. This is because a simple, clear interface was common to people throughout the world and because the project was spread through participants' blogs.

Since it's best to produce a system in which users themselves can continuously create the value of contents, it was essential to produce a community-like site to realize this purpose. Entries by such large numbers of users will increase the number of trees planted and allow them to enjoy reading many entries from around the world.

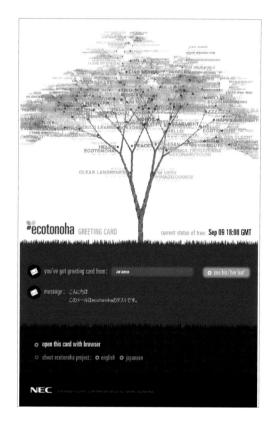

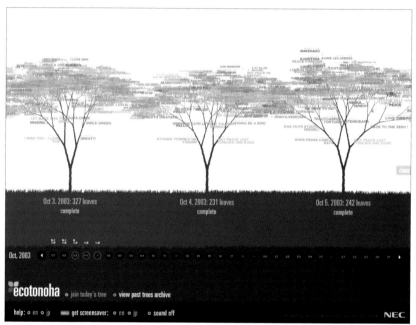

Users transform the tree on the Web by posting messages. As part of the campaign, a real tree was planted on an island in Australia for every hundred visitors to the site. Over 600 trees were given a new life as a result of the site from July to December of 2003.

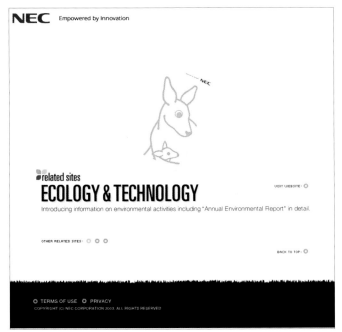

NEC Empowered by Innovation

related sites
ECOLOGY & TECHNOLOGY

VISIT WEBSITE :

Introducing information on environmental activities including "Annual Environmental Report" in detail.

OTHER RELATED SITES :

BACK TO TOP :

TERMS OF USE   PRIVACY
COPYRIGHT (C) NEC CORPORATION 2003. ALL RIGHTS RESERVED

NEC Empowered by Innovation

ecotonoha
THE WORD TREE WHICH BRINGS GREENERY TO LIFE

enter - fullscreen
enter - normal

ECOTONOHA IS A PROJECT - TO NURTURE A VIRTUAL TREE COLLABORATIVELY, AND AT THE SAME TIME CONTRIBUTE TO THE ACTUAL ENVIRONMENT TO COPE WITH GLOBAL WARMING. AS YOU MAKE ECOTONOHA'S LEAVES, THE VIRTUAL TREE WILL GROW, AND AS ECOTONOHA GROWS, REAL TREES WILL BE PLANTED BY NEC.

about ecotonoha

- HOW TO PARTICIPATE
- REAL TREES WILL GROW TOO
- SIGNATURE RESTRICTIONS
- CREATOR'S PROFILE
- HOW TO MAKE A LINK
- CONTACT
- NOTE
- BEST VIEWED WITH

information

- 07.14.2003 : ECOTONOHA PROJECT STARTED
- 07.22.2003 : ARCHIVE TREES RELEASED

TERMS OF USE   PRIVACY
COPYRIGHT (C) NEC CORPORATION 2003. ALL RIGHTS RESERVED

NEC Empowered by Innovation

AdNEC **N SQUARE**

→ Home   → Mr.N   → Project   → Advertising   → Event   → Coffee Break   → Link   → IT Keywords

ENGLISH

ecotonoha
緑を生みだす言葉の樹

enter - fullscreen
enter - normal

ecotonoha [エコトノハ] は、みんなでインターネットの樹を育て、現実の森を創っていく参加型プロジェクト。
あなたも一緒にecotonohaで地球のみどりをひろげてみませんか？

about ecotonoha

- 参加するには
- バーチャルからリアルへ
- 書き込みは1日1回
- CREATOR'S PROFILE
- LINKするには
- CONTACT
- 推奨環境

information

- 07.14.2003 : エコトノハプロジェクトをスタートしました。

Copyright(C) NEC Corporation 2003

このサイトについて   Sitemap   お問い合わせ

Pencil Winners

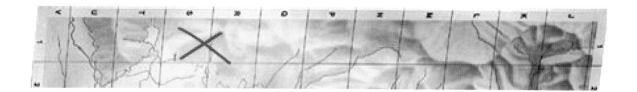

MAPPING OUT A SUCCESSFUL BANNER AD

To exhibit the boundless possibilities available to drivers with Audi's unique allroad® technology, the creative team at AlmapBBDO utilized Flash to build a winning, drop-down map that perfectly captured the client's brief.

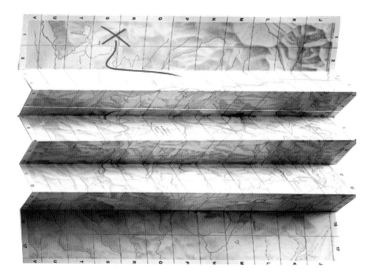

Art Directors:
Luiz Sanches, Adriel Nunes
Writer:
Tales Bahu
Programmer:
Paulo Pacheco
Creative Directors:
Marcello Serpa, Fabio Costa
URL:
http://www.almapbbdo.com.br/
awards/2004/audi/cabriolet/
ID:
04001N

How did the fact that the banner was covering screen content affect the process?

This format—an expanding banner—is very common and successful in Brazil. As long as the content on the screen is covered only with the user's intervention (mouse over the closed banner), there's no problem at all with this process. It's just like a Web site menu that works with mouse over. Technically speaking, it's a work produced in Flash that allows everyone with version 6.0 to see it.

What was the inspiration behind the piece?

The main characteristic of Audi allroad® is its good performance on all kinds of roads: on road and off road. Keeping this in mind, the art director's idea was to show this feature by communicating that with this car, you can travel around every place in the world, with no need to change the type of car.

How did the client respond to the work?
How did users respond?

The client quickly approved the work, since it shows exactly the concept of this car. It seems that the users liked it as well, since its click-through rate was 2.1%, a very good rate for a non-promotional/sale work.

AGENCY AlmapBBDO/São Paulo
CLIENT Audi

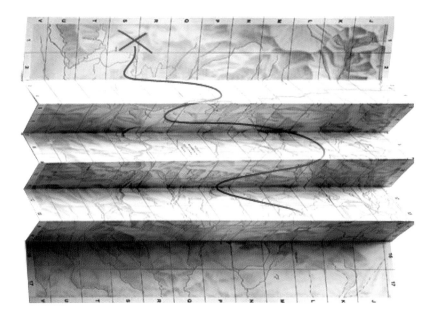

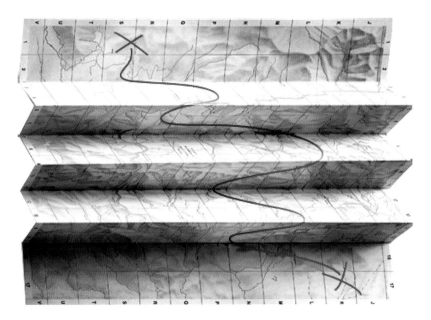

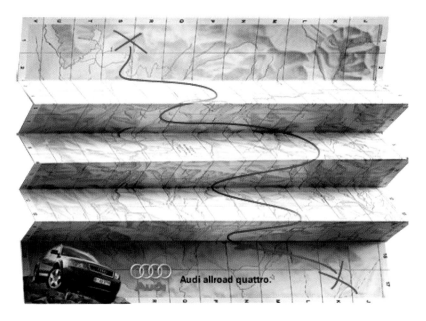

A SHOCK AND AWE-INSPIRING BANNER

Through the use of a shockingly simple execution, the creative team at Brazil's AlmapBBDO was able to effortlessly show users the benefit of Mizuno's Wave Shock Absorption System.

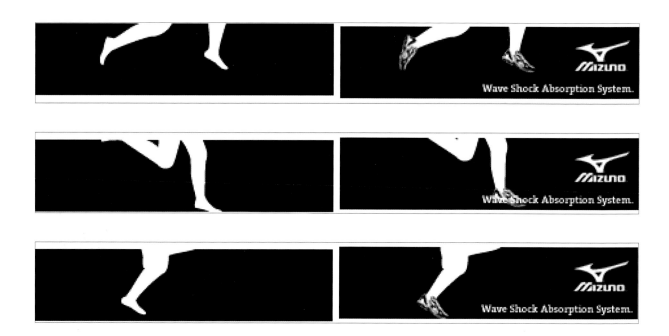

Art Director:
Eduardo Foresti
Writer:
Bruno Godinho
Creative Directors:
Fabio Costa, Eduardo Foresti
URL:
http://www.almapbbdo.com.br/
awards/2004/mizuno/half
ID:
04002N

What was the client's brief?
The brief was to communicate through the Internet the new shoe technology, Mizuno Wave Shock Absorption System.

The execution is really innovative. What were the challenges?
The full banner format is very limited in terms of technical specifications. The challenge was to use this format in a different way, and at the same time, make it simple. The concept to be communicated was that the wave shock absorption system solves a specific problem, as you can see through the animation.

What was the click-through rate?
The average rate was 1%.

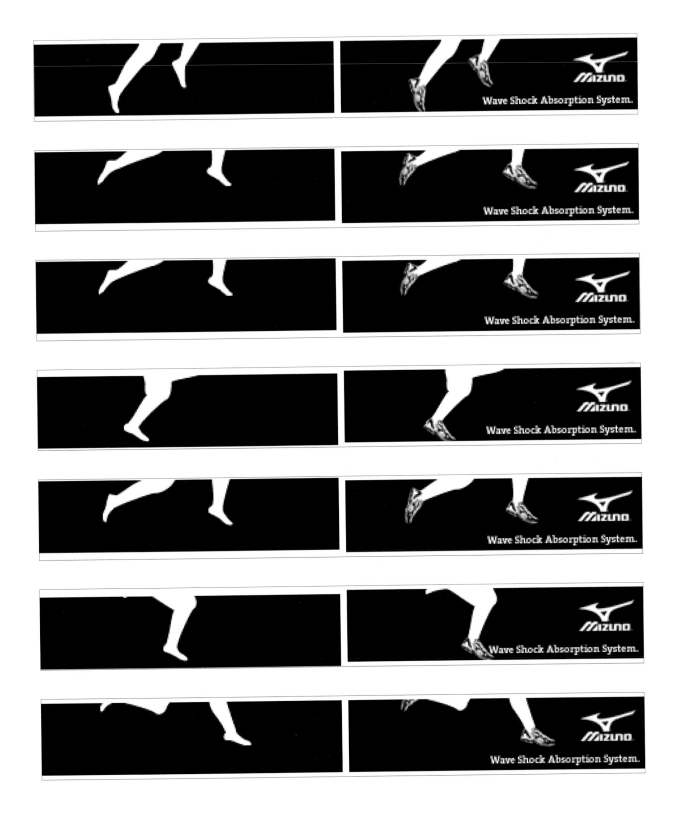

What was the objective of the campaign?

The main objective was to make the audience go through an adventure to discover our Adventure Channel. It also gave us a great opportunity to "teach" the real spirit of an explorer.

Talk about the technical execution.

In order to give the sensation that you were really climbing the rock, this interactive ad was entirely made and programmed in Macromedia Flash. So, after shooting all the arm positions, we put it together with the background, animated the flag frame by frame, and finally, added the sound of the scream.

How have users responded?
What audience was the campaign directed toward?

As this campaign was targeted for people who really love extreme sports, the response couldn't have been better. The number of visitors increased and we've even received some e-mails with congratulations for the "lesson."

Art Director:
Eco Moliterno
Writers:
Eco Moliterno, Luli Radfahrer
Programmer:
Marcelo Nishio
Producer:
Eco Moliterno
Designer:
Eco Moliterno
Creative Director:
Luli Radfahrer
URL:
www.aol.com.br/midiakit/
festivais/adventure
ID:
04003N

agency AOL Brazil/São Paulo
client AOL Brazil

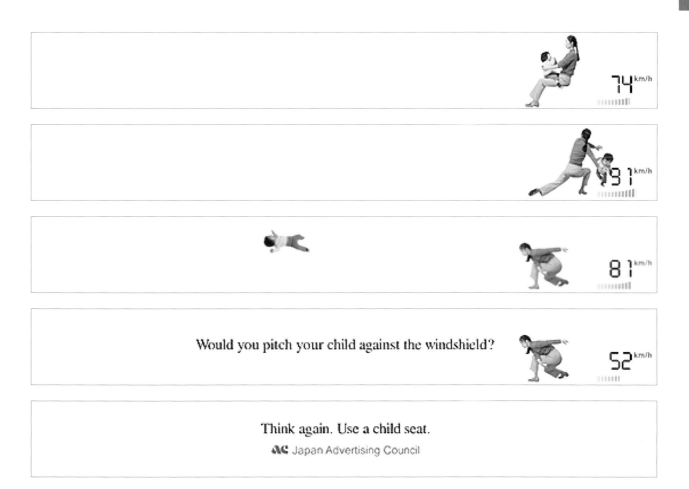

Would you pitch your child against the windshield?

Think again. Use a child seat.

AC Japan Advertising Council

The banner has a powerful message.
How did the creative team come up with this concept?
We first defined the framework of the message as, "A parent who does not use a child seat is endangering his or her child." Then we discussed how to deliver this message to the audience effectively, and we developed several plans. Among them, this was the simplest and the most straightforward idea. Accordingly, it is fair to say that the message assumed a quite important role in the production of this banner ad.

Was there any adverse reaction to the banner?
During the production process, we had heated discussions about one question that was raised: "Isn't this image of a mother pitching her child cruel and unacceptable?" This issue created a more serious situation inside our company than we could have ever imagined. However, the client consistently supported our plan and helped us overcome the problem. In addition to the One Show, the banner ad won a Tokyo Interactive Ad Award (TIAA) and a prize at Cannes. After these commendations, we began to receive feedback from concerned parties in related industries and from viewers. As we were not aware of any reaction from our audience when the banner was first displayed, we recognized that getting the attention of society through the secondary exposure made possible by winning prizes is also an important opportunity for communication.

Art Directors:
Hirozumi Takakusaki, Aya Sakagami
Writer:
Shoichi Tamura
Photographer/Illustrator:
Shoji Ishikawa
Programmer:
Atsushi Motomura
Producers:
Masataka Hosogane, Masayoshi Boku
Designer:
Aya Sakagami
Creative Directors:
Shoichi Tamura, Makoto Teramoto
URL:
www.interactive-salaryman.com/
2004pieces/d0306E/
ID:
04004N

GRINNING AND BEARING IT ON THE WEB

DoubleYou Barcelona unleashed a rabid pack of digital bears to successfully advertise the 2003 San Silvestre Vallecana Race campaign for Nike and provide users with an innovative — and welcome — on-screen intrusion.

Art Director:
Anna Coll
Writers:
Eduard Pou, Joakim Borgström, Oriol Villar
Programmers:
Joakim Borgström, Mauricio Mazzariol
Digital Artist/Multimedia:
Mauricio Mazzariol
Producer:
Jordi Pont
Designer:
Anna Coll
Creative Directors:
Eduard Pou, Joakim Borgström, Oriol Villar
URL:
http://www.doubleyou.com/festivals/
nikesansilvestre/oneshow2.html
ID:
04005N

Can you describe some of the technical challenges and successes of the piece?
It may sound weird but the most difficult technical problem we had was to find a real way to animate the bear. We tried to make it run with some animation programs but it was impossible. We hardly managed to make it walk; it looked more like a robot than a bear. So after watching some DVDs about bears, we found a part with 12 frames of a baby bear. We enlarged the head and touched up the frames to achieve the same rhythm as the runner.

Was it a concern to you that one of the banners would cover a significant portion of on-screen content?
I don't think it's terribly unpleasant to watch a runner who is pursued by bears, at least for a moment. Also, there isn't any advertising text that tries to sell something. Actually, we are against intrusive advertising, but I believe that in this case, due to the mark of the swoosh of Nike, users are more biased to watch our pieces.

AGENCY DoubleYou/Barcelona
client American Nike

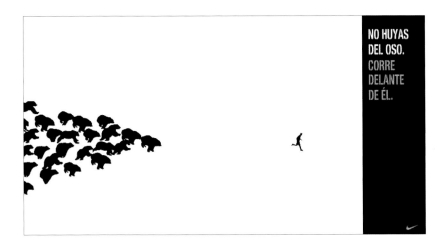

Talk a little about the agency/client relationship and how it resulted in this award-winning work.

The 2003 San Silvestre Vallecana Race campaign for Nike is an example of an integrated campaign, where the client met with its offline agency Villar & Rosàs, its media companies Media Planning and Media Contacts and its interactive advertising agency DoubleYou. Each of us worked from his or her field on the concept that the offline agency came up with, which was a bear walking free in Madrid. On the Internet, we developed two complementary lines of thinking. One was about a runner who used the fact he was being chased by bears as a perfect excuse to run. The site had a very emotional language in which the music and the sound effects played key roles. It was possible for users, among other things, to register online for the San Silvestre race, know the running products of the brand, or send an ironic piece of viral marketing where you must escape from the bear.

The second line was more underground. It deals with the urban legend from a more humorous point of view and it was based on viral pieces generated by a false group of citizens who wanted to hunt the bear. Its purpose was just to generate rumors about the story used in the campaign.

more >>

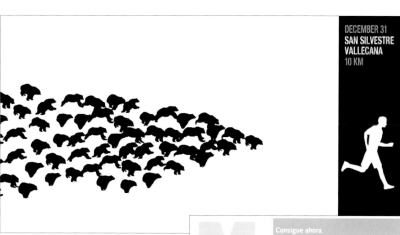

SI LO VES, CORRE

A HOLIDAY CAMPAIGN WITHOUT THE CLUTTER

Goodby, Silverstein & Partners incorporated the playful nature of iconic holiday imagery into a series of four whimsical online activities aimed to draw users to Discover's Gift Finder microsite.

Have a jolly holiday, but please drive carefully.

AUTOSTEER ON   It pays to DISCOVER

Art Director:
Will McGinness
Writer:
Jody Horn
Production Company:
The Barbarian Group
Producer:
Kris Smith
Creative Director:
Keith Anderson
URL:
http://www.goodbysilverstein.com/
awards/discovercard
ID:
04006N

Talk a little about the creative process and the production of the banners. What were some of the technical challenges?
With an increasingly savvy and time-pressed online audience already inundated by loud, hollow holiday messages, we felt our best chance of getting users to click through was to charm shoppers with genuine, playful banners that captured the spirit of the holidays.

What was the client's brief?
We were asked to build a campaign that would break through the clutter of holiday advertising in the online space and invite users to visit the Discover Card Gift Finder microsite,

How did users react?
What was the click through-rate on the banners?
Our confidentiality agreement with the client does not allow us to disclose this information.

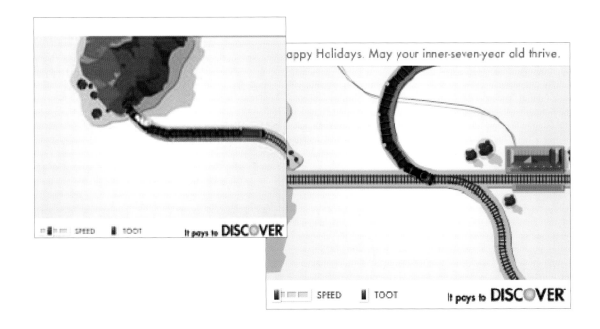

COMMUNICATING THE STYLE OF STILO

Asked by the client to emphasize the improvements made to the Fiat Stilo, AgênciaClick navigates within the page to go outside of the box.

Sky Window. Either you have it, or you don't.
Fiat STILO

Sky Window. Either you have it, or you don't.
Fiat STILO

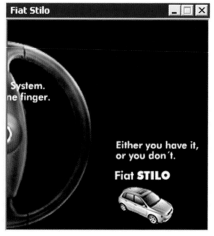

Driving is an interactive experience.
Did you strive to reflect this in the banner ads?
Actually, this campaign wasn't about driving, but about the few (and not so few) technological improvements that made Stilo one of the most developed models in its category. This campaign was created to explore these new technologies launched in the Fiat Stilo, treating them as unique strengths of the car and letting the user experience them.

What were the technical challenges in creating this campaign?
The biggest challenge was coming up with different ideas to highlight each feature that would let the user try out the new technology. Each feature got a different piece—all of them were created individually and programmed to provide the most vivid experience. Some of them were easier to develop, such as the wheel that you turn with a "finger." Others weren't so technologically difficult, but it took a huge effort to convince the clients to let us navigate within the pages. But the worst to develop was the scrolling piece that never touches the lower arrow, for the parking sensor. It was a nightmare that turned into a dream when it finally worked!

Art Directors:
Rodrigo Buim, Veni Cury, Emerson Viegas
Writers:
Veni Cury, Emerson Viegas
Programmer:
Vagner Monteiro
Producer:
Luciana Braga
Designers:
Veni Cury, Emerson Viegas, Vagner Monteiro
Creative Director:
PJ Pereira
URL:
http://awards.agenciaclick.com.br/
stiloexperience/en
ID:
04007N

AGENCY AgênciaClick/São Paulo
CLIENT Fiat Stilo-Brasil

How did the client respond to the work?

How did users respond?

They bought the idea since the very first presentation, but when we launched it, the feedback was even more impressive than we thought. We received lots of congratulating e-mails and so did the client. A couple of months later we realized that car buyers remembered most of the features presented in this online campaign and nowhere else! A year later, whenever we get briefs, people still say, "We thought you might come up with something as bright as that Stilo campaign..."

GOING ONLINE
WITH A BANG

The relationship between Hewlett-Packard, Bang & Olufsen and Goodby, Silverstein & Partners leads to a Web-based voice recognition banner that really has people talking.

HP servers help Bang & Olufsen create audio/video innovations that look as great as they sound.

Art Director:
Jeff Benjamin
Writers:
Peter Albores, Peter Rudy
Production Companies:
Natzke Design, Oddcast
Producer:
Mike Geiger
Creative Directors:
Steve Simpson, Keith Anderson
URL:
http://www.goodbysilverstein.com/
awards/hp/interactive
ID:
04008N

Discuss the successful relationship between HP and Bang & Olufsen.
Every day Bang & Olufsen receives thousands of product orders from around the world. More than 60 percent of them arrive via the company's Global Retail System. Bang & Olufsen relies on HP ProLiant servers to form the server backbone not only for its Global Retail System, but for every one of its new production platforms. This reliance on HP technology extends to the Internet, where HP ProLiant servers enpower the Bang & Olufsen Web site.

What were some of the technical considerations with the banners, specifically with the voice-recognition visualizer banner?
The main challenge was getting the voice recorded so that it could be played in the banner via a phone call. This required a lot of server communication. First, the banner the user had on their screen had to be identified. This was overcome by giving each viewer their own identification number that they would enter in after they called the number they saw in the banner. Once they entered that number and recorded their voice, the banner knew which audio file to pull from the server. On the server, frequency values for the sounds were retrieved, which were then later visualized in the banner using Flash to animate these sound waves.

How did users react?
Was the click-through rate what you expected?
We can probably say it was very successful and people were amazed to hear their own voice and see the animation in the banner. We were actually surprised how many people clicked through the banner and tested it.

AGENCY Goodby, Silverstein & Partners/San Francisco
client Hewlett-Packard

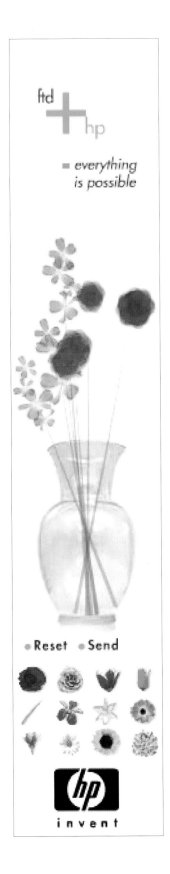

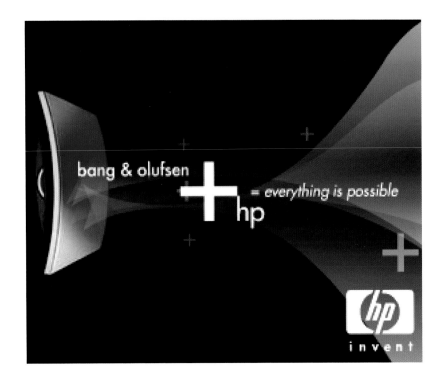

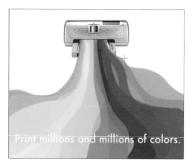

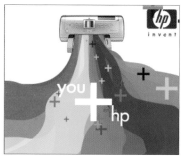

Art Director:
John Nussbaum
Writer:
Aaron Griffiths
Production Company:
Natzke Design
Producer:
Amanda Kelso
Creative Directors:
Steve Simpson, Keith Anderson
URL:
http://www.goodbysilverstein.com/
awards/hp/you
ID:
04009N

What was the client's brief and how was it executed?
We needed to position HP as a leader in digital photography and do it in a way that demonstrated quality and understanding of the subject. As proof, we felt it was important to use high-quality photographs in most of the ads. We also needed to devise interactions that would demonstrate the clear advantages of digital vs. traditional photographs (e.g. changeable, interactive, portable).

Discuss the technical challenges of the banners.
File size is always a challenge. But when you're given the task to animate high-quality, photographic images, the file size constraint becomes a virtual death grip. Ads like these require the kind of Flash that you don't read about in a book. With most of the work we do for HP, we are forced to use the technology in a way it hasn't been used before.

HP and Goodby, Silverstein & Partners have a rich tradition of creative online work. How did the team look to expand upon that with these banners?
This assignment was different in that it dealt with a very real, very tangible product category. Therefore, the ads themselves needed to be felt, not just experienced. It became extremely important that people were immersed in not only the ad, but also the brave new world of digital photography.

AGENCY Goodby, Silverstein & Partners/San Francisco
client Hewlett-Packard

Discuss some of the technical issues of the execution.
In order to visualize the atmosphere of the Aichi EXPO 2005, the designer focused on the idea of events occuring in nature by applying them to Action Script.

Discuss your approach to the art direction/creative aesthetic of the banners.
The theme of this exposition focuses on nature. However, the banners not only represent the beauty of nature, but they create an illusion of the natural world where visitors can feel the atmosphere and closeness of it. In our everyday life, we tend to neglect all of the precious and small creatures living around us. Through these banners, we sincerely hope that the visitors will appreciate their existence and rediscover their magnificent beauty.

What was the client's brief?
The series of interactive banners were designed to promote EXPO 2005 in Aichi, Japan. The subject for this exposition features "Wisdom in Nature" that introduces the ideal methods of helping the creation of a better world where the human civilization and the natural environment can co-exist in harmony. The banner interaction provides a platform where visitors can interact with "Wisdom in Nature" on a virtual level and take a moment to rediscover the wonder in nature.

Art Director:
Tadaaki Harada
Writers:
Toshiya Fukuda, Junya Masuda,
Michael Glenn
Photographers/Illustrators:
Tadaaki Harada, Junya Masuda
Programmers:
Tadaaki Harada, Takeshiro Umetsu
Digital Artists/Multimedia:
Tadaaki Harada, Takeshiro Umetsu
Agency Producers:
Tatsuya Sagitani, Masayo Ito
Production Company:
Hakuhodo i-studio
Producer:
Tomohiro Shinoda
Designer:
Tadaaki Harada
Information Architect:
Toshiya Fukuda
Creative Directors:
Noboru Inoue, Toshiya Fukuda
URL:
http://award.i-studio.co.jp/2004_expo/
01.html,02.html,03.html,04.html
ID:
04010N

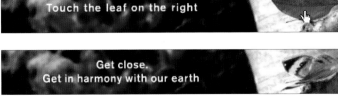

A HOLIDAY SHOPPING DISCOVERY

The goal of the Discover Card Gift Finder was to create a fun shopping experience with an "anti-retail" feel by providing help only when asked. How's that for quality customer service?

Talk a little about the creative process and the production of the banners.

Looking to capitalize on the online holiday shopping sales spike, our client asked us to create a banner campaign that would encourage people to pay for their gift purchases with the Discover Card. Instead, we suggested that the best way to get people to use their Discover Card when buying presents was to create our own gift site.

Talk a little bit about the execution.

Our goal was to simplify the many hassles of holiday shopping and enhance all that was fun about it. The Gift Finder generates gift ideas based on very basic criteria: the age and hobbies of recipients and desired price range. It has an "anti-retail" mentality that provides help only when asked and a printable shopping list function to keep track of various recipients' gift ideas. And finally, what holiday shopping spree would be complete without department store muzak?

The Flash for the site is integrated with a custom J2EE/Tomcat back-end and an SQL database for storing and retrieving gifts and gift information, as well as for e-mail services.

Art Director:
Will McGinness
Writer:
Jody Horn
Production Company:
The Barbarian Group
Producer:
Mike Geiger
Creative Director:
Keith Anderson
URL:
http://www.goodbysilverstein.com/awards/discovercard
ID:
04012N

agency Goodby, Silverstein & Partners/San Francisco
client Discover Card

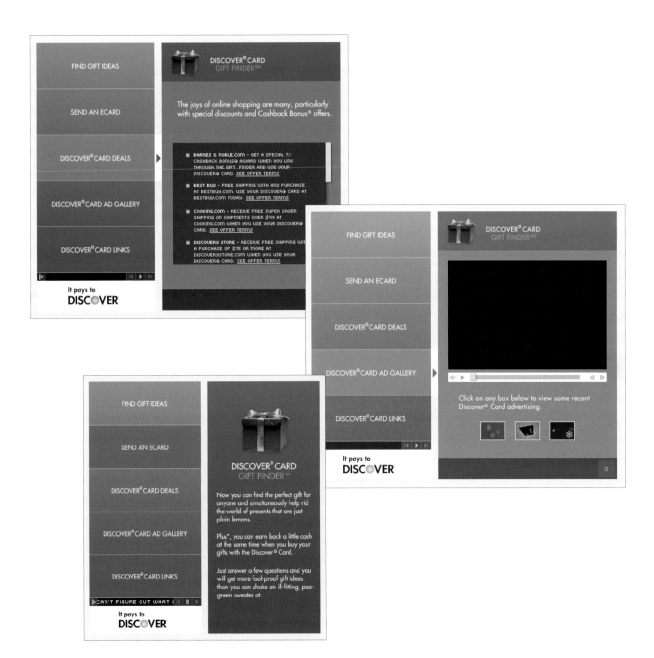

THE FLASH AND FLARE OF THE X5 EXPERIENCE

Herraiz Soto & Co. accepted the challenge set by BMW to create a site that would generate excitement in the consumer on an emotional level. To achieve this, they utilized the flexibility and capability of Flash MX to creative a sense of digital freedom.

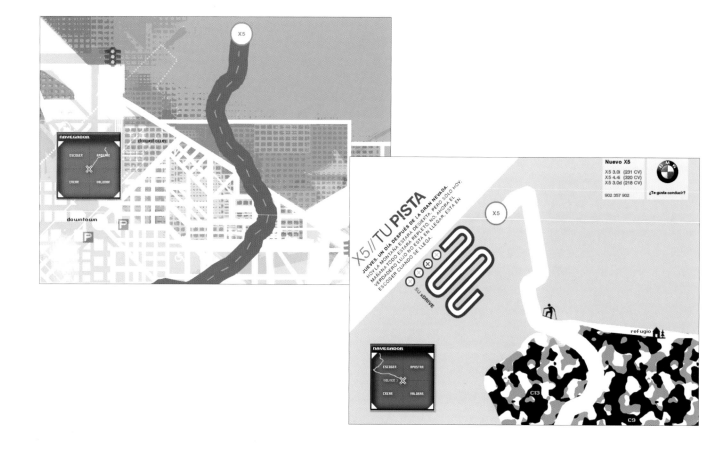

Discuss some of the technical issues of the execution and the importance of user interaction in automotive Web sites.
Behind the purchase of a car there are rational as well as emotional elements. The easy part in presenting an automobile is to demonstrate its technical specifications, its exterior design and its features. Good production alone is quite sufficient when it comes to putting these details across in a coherent fashion. What is genuinely difficult is to create communication that will excite a consumer on an emotional level. And that is precisely where we believe the success of a Web site about cars is to be found. Interactive media constitutes an extremely powerful tool for creating emotions, and in this piece we wished to transmit the sensations that off-road driving offers, notwithstanding the fact that this is an eminently comfortable and elegant car. To achieve this, we combined the sensation of freedom, which you get from going where you want, with elegant peaceful music to transmit calm and confidence. The piece was entirely produced by using Flash MX.

Art Directors:
Angel Herraiz, Sergi Mula
Programmers:
Carles Sanz, Genis Bayarri
Creative Directors:
Angel Herraiz, Rafa Soto
URL:
http://www.herraizsoto.com/
festivales/X5web
ID:
04013N

Agency Herraiz Soto & Co./Barcelona
client BMW

What was the client's brief?
How did they respond to the finished product?

The brief given by the client was to communicate the characteristics of the car, and to relate them to the lifestyle of the consumer, who is a mature, urban male who has already achieved something in his life. This is a man, therefore, who is capable of appreciating good things in life, and one of these good things is the BMW X5. Moreover, the BMW X5 should communicate the sensation of highly enjoyable driving, since the car is capable of allowing the driver to feel all the characteristics and textures of the terrain in addition to conferring an extraordinary level of driving safety.

The response of the client to our proposal was positive. They were particularly allured by the capacity of a piece to transmit part of the experience of driving, which is much more difficult to achieve without interactive media.

How did users respond?

Sixty percent of the users reached the four destinations and the average browsing time was around eight minutes. In addition to this, and in the course of an internal test, we observed how the user, apart from a concrete destination, takes pleasure in driving for the sake of driving, for the simple pleasure of feeling the experience.

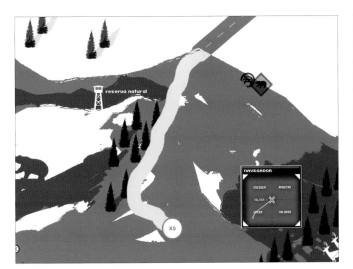

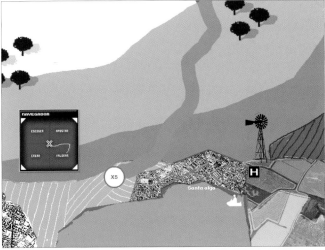

SPECIALIZING IN ONLINE TECHNICAL OBSESSION

Known for their attention to technical and design detail, Specialized hired Goodby, Silverstein & Partners to build a site that went beyond a simple, rotating 3-D showroom and exhibited the company's unique eye for innovation.

What was the client's brief and how did you successfully execute it?
Specialized wanted to reclaim its rightful position as the most technically obsessed bike manufacturer in the world. In both the print and Web executions, we focused on the intricate details of Specialized's most recent innovations.

What were some of the technical considerations with the microsites?
To stake their ground as a technological innovator, it was crucial that every component of each experience be technically precise. This meant using the most advanced technologies to ensure the experiences would be as easy to use as possible.

Discuss the art direction and how you wanted the microsites to look as compared to other sites for bicycles.
There are good bike sites and bad bike sites. Our goal was neither. We just cracked open Specialized and let their passion pour out. We don't think we ended up with Web sites. They just are what they are—raw, passionate, and kinda funny—the embodiment of Specialized.

Art Directors:
Steve Mapp, John Nussbaum, Jon Soto, Jack Woodworth
Writers:
Aaron Griffiths, Al Kelly
Photographer/Illustrator:
Dan Escobar
Production Company:
Kurt Noble
Producer:
Kris Smith
Creative Director:
Rich Silverstein
URL:
http://www.goodbysilverstein.com/awards/specialized_microsites
ID:
04014N

AGENCY Goodby, Silverstein & Partners/San Francisco
client Specialized

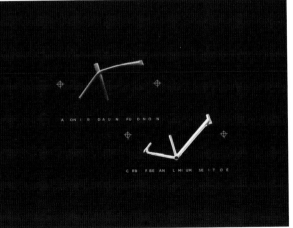

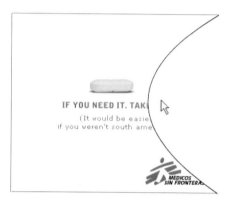

A BORDER BETWEEN HELPLESSNESS AND HOPE

SIGN NOW AGAINST BARRIERS TO ESSENTIAL MEDICINES

What was the objective of this piece?
To obtain signs to avoid the FTAA treatment comes into force. To inform about the restrictions people from Latin America would have to get some basic medicines if the FTAA treatment came into force.

Talk about the technical execution.
The entire purpose of the technical execution is to make the user feel, through an interactive experience, the helplessness of wanting to reach something and realizing it is impossible for him. Once he assumes he cannot reach what he wants, by interacting with the campaign, the user goes to the microsite where he can easily demolish all these barriers that the FTAA intends to build up to prevent people from some countries of Latin America to have access to basic medicine. This is a simple execution focused on people who can internalize the message through an interactive experience and communicate the message through interactivity.

How have users responded?
What audience was the site directed towards?
This is a global campaign launched in several countries simultaneously. All the countries used the same creativity except for Spain, where we created a specific campaign. More than the 80% of the global response came from the campaign and microsite developed in Spain.

Art Director:
Susana Romero
Writer:
Javier G. Patiño
Programmers:
Raúl Fernández, Alejandro Harto
Agency Producer:
Carlos Wassmann
Creative Directors:
Juan Luis Bastos, Javier G. Patiño
URL:
http://www.zentropyspain.com/festivals/msf
ID:
04015N

Agency ZENTROPY/Madrid
client MSF España

THE DIGITAL HEART AND SOUL OF MITSUBISHI

Incorporating highly stylized art direction, Dentsu effectively uses the Lancer Evolution to drive us out of the "Sluggish Life" and into the "Heart Beat World" of Mitsubishi Motors.

shake the mouse

Art Directors:
Takeshi Mizukawa, Kentaro Suda,
Doris Fuerst, Malte Haust, Lars Eberle
Writers:
Takeshi Mizukawa, Bernd Muller,
Morgan Bell
Digital Artists/Multimedia:
Marcus Kirsch, Thomas Meyer,
Vassilios Alexiou
Agency Producers:
Katsuhiko Iwasaki, Tomoko Kobayashi
Production Companies:
Aoi Advertising Promotion, Less Rain
Producers:
Kumiko Kitamura, Tetsuya Yamada
Designers:
Ron Jonzo, Oliver Greschke
Creative Directors:
Satoshi Nakajima, Lars Eberle
URL:
www.i-shake-u.com
ID: 04016N

The Web site has both a contemporary and retro feel. Describe the creative process with regard to the site's art direction?

We did not focus on the fusion between contemporary and retro feels. However, the theme for the Web site was to get out or break out from "Sluggish Life," and in order to feature this symbolic scene, we introduced the image of decadent urban civilizations, which was represented in the '60s and '70s. That's why we focused on a retro tone for the first half of the scene. Since we wanted the last half of the scene, which introduces "Real Heart Beat," to highlight animal instincts, we designed with the motif such as jungle filled with vivid colors.

agency Dentsu/Tokyo
client Mitsubishi Motors Corporation

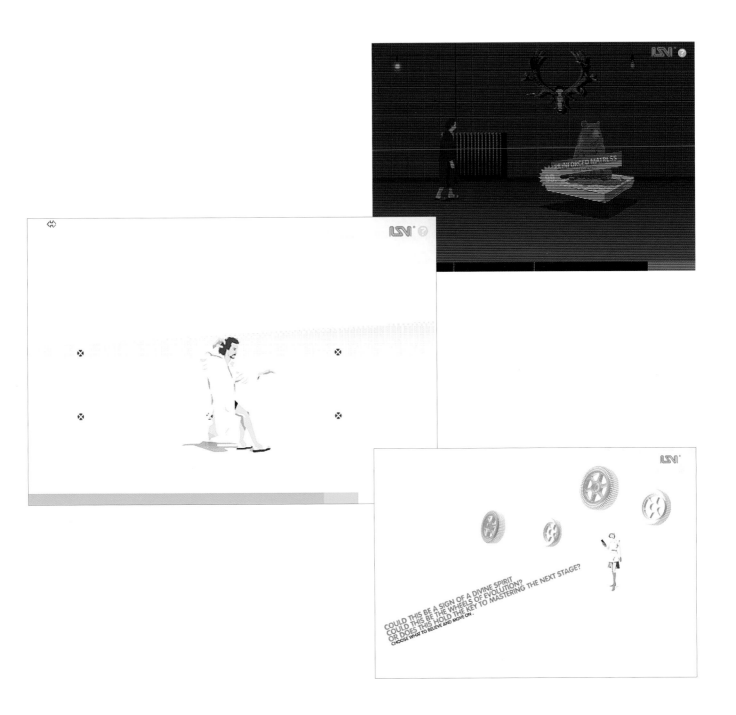

Talk about the client's brief and discuss your success in translating the client's ideas.

The client, Mitsubishi Motors Corporation, asked us to produce a Web site that introduces their corporate slogan, "Heart Beat Motors," as well as provides the opportunity for users to experience the slogan. To achieve this, we came up with a basic story: The main character Todd, who goofs off everyday, is to be influenced by a flagship car called Lancer Evolution and he gets out from the "Sluggish Life" and discovers "Hear Beat World." In order to maximize users' "Real Heart Beat" experience, we did not provide any instructions on how to play the game. This way, users gradually figure out the trick of clicking with the beat to clear the stages. As one finds the beat of the background music, the music gets nicer, and the game generates more excitement. Without realizing it, users eventually reach the highest stage of the game, which introduces the world of "Heart Beat."

more >>

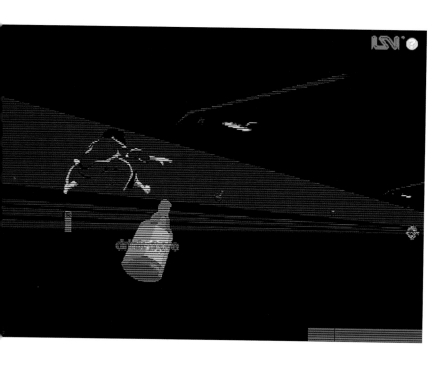

AGENCY Dentsu/Tokyo
CLIENT Mitsubishi Motors Corporation

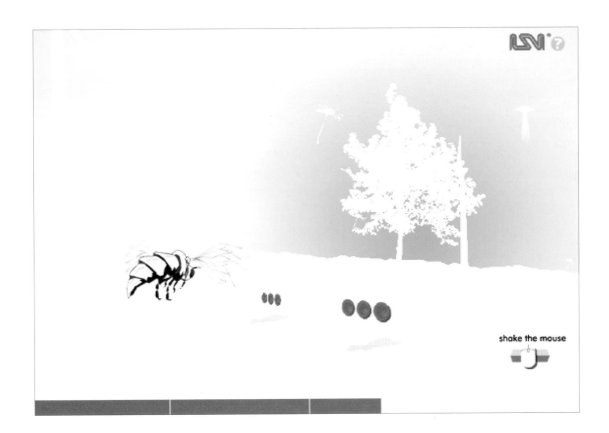

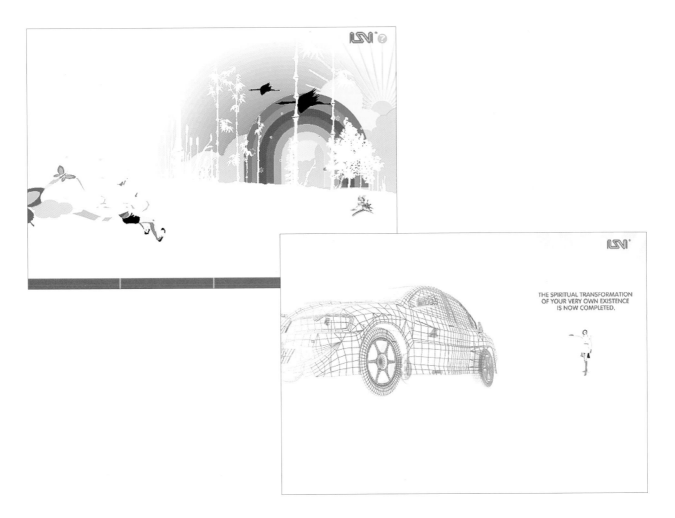

AN ORIGINAL IDEA REBORN ONLINE

As the very first online regional project for Levi's, OgilvyOne worldwide conceived a Web site encompassing the concept of creative rebirth through strong design and interactivity.

Art Directors:
Ashidiq Ghazali, Dominic Goldman
Writer:
Audra Tan
Programmers:
Chandra Barathi, Dara Lim, Colin Foo,
Raju TV, Ronnie Liew
Producer:
Yow Pin Fern
Designers:
Ashidiq Ghazali, Dominic Goldman,
Arnold Widjanarko, Shawn Loo
Creative Director:
Dominic Goldman
URL:
http://www.our-work.com/levis/
site/index_main.html
ID:
04017N

Can you talk about some of the technical issues and objectives of the site?

One main objective is to ensure that the site runs as efficiently and reliably as possible so that the user's experience is enhanced while navigating through it. Web assets are optimized to ensure minimal waiting periods for downloads on this highly interactive site. In order to further improve the user's experience, we split the site into two sections: high bandwidth and low bandwidth. This enables visual throttling without sacrificing the experience for a wide range of users. The applications are also optimized for faster processing and database connectivity to ensure that it is able to handle the expected traffic to the site. In addition, the site uses soundtracks that are streamed from a dedicated streaming server.

AGENCY OgilvyOne worldwide/Singapore
CLIENT Levi Strauss

What was the inspiration behind the art direction of the site?
The brief was to develop an online campaign for the original 501 jean that had been re-cut. Based on the proposition of "501 Reborn," the site was conceptualized with the visual of an adult crouched in a fetal position as the creative idea. This would act as the main navigation of the site and work in various ways as sub navigations.

How did the client respond to the work?
How did users respond?
The clients were very pleased with the work developed. The 501 Reborn microsite is the very first online project for Levi's on a regional basis. Individual markets like Korea and Malaysia were enthusiastic in their responses and quickly adopted the regional site, keeping its overall look and main elements while adapting it with localized content. Based on the results, users spent a reasonable amount of time on the site interacting especially with viral elements like the music mixer. Using one of any three Marvin Gaye tracks, this allowed them to create their own mix and send it on to their friends. Users also loved the free downloads of wallpapers and screensavers. Overall, the site gained a lot of positive feedback with its strong design and interactivity.

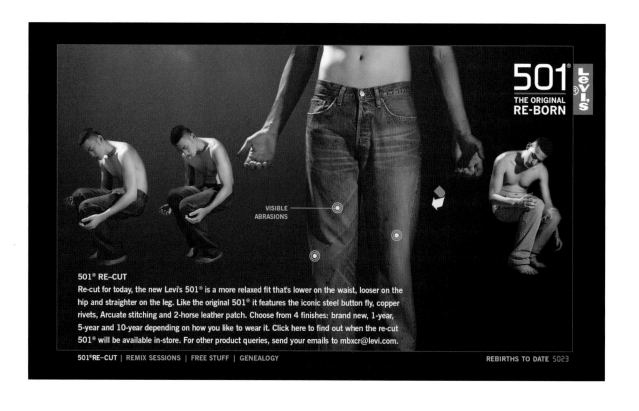

agency OgilvyOne worldwide/Singapore
client Levi Strauss

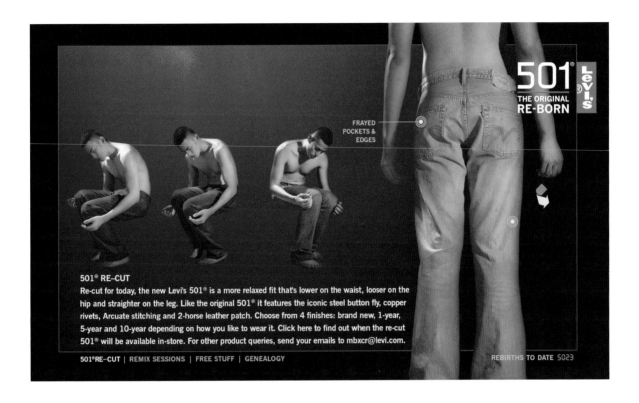

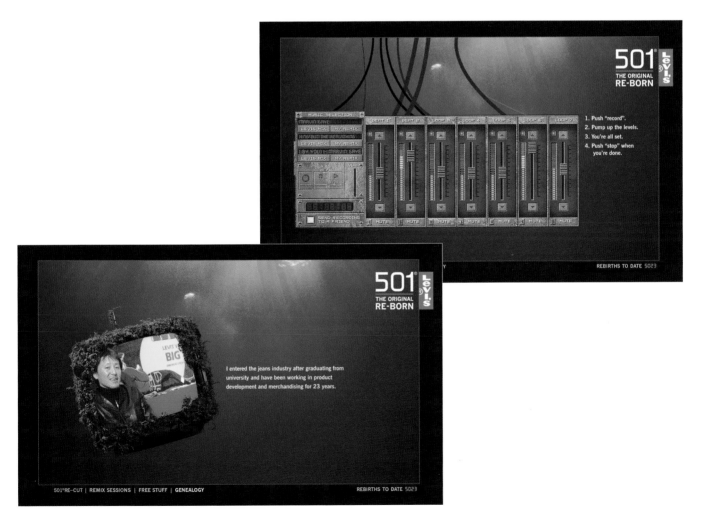

THE KEYS TO CAPTURING AN ARTISTS WEB IDENTITY

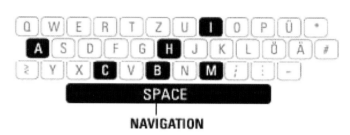

Can you talk about some of the technical issues?
There is a lot of multimedia content on the site.
It was really a technical challenge to integrate the high-quality and rather large video sequences from the music video into a Flash Web site that has data size and performance restrictions. The "Flash-Typo Engine" is a technical highlight in that a randomly generated song lyric renews the design page-view per page-view.

What was the inspiration behind the piece?
How much of the design reflects the artist's personality?
Naturally, Sabrina's music, lyrics, and personality should be the focus of the site. That's why the keypad navigation only appears when it is needed. Our main goal was to present Sabrina in an interactive fashion on the Web site to satisfy her fans.

How did the client respond to the work?
How did users respond?
Sabrina and the label were both incredibly pleased with the finished work. We were able to exceed even their highest expectations. The users were also very impressed with the site: the new Sabrina site was a hot topic for months on the label's online user forum.

Art Director:
Bejadin Selimi
Writer:
Katarina Steinijans
Creative Director:
Olaf Czeschner
URL:
http://www.neue-digitale.de/
awards/sabrina.html
ID:
04018N

agency Neue Digitale/Frankfurt am Main
client 3p Pelham Power Production

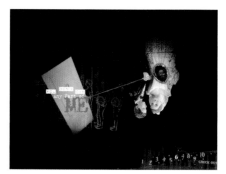

How important was it for the interactivity to reflect the twisting plotline of the film?

Sony Pictures made it clear that they wanted the marketing for the *Identity* movie to be more a "what is it" than a "whodunnit." So, the Web site needed to abandon the actual story and focus on fragmenting the film's calm chaotic visual and aural atmosphere. By chopping up the material into small moments, it forced the Internet audience to continue interacting with the site for clues when we gave none.

What were the technical challenges in creating this campaign?

The main technical challenge in building the Identity site was to deal with sound. We wanted to have full control over ambient sounds and music, independent of timeline-based animations. This resulted in the creation of a code library for handling sounds that we have used on every site we have made since then.

Art Director:
Richard Foster
Programmer:
Joshua Hirsch
Digital Artists/Multimedia:
Richard Foster, D. Garrett Nantz,
George Ernst, Dexter Cruz,
Frank Campanella
Designers:
George Ernst, Richard Foster, Dexter Cruz,
D. Garrett Nantz
Creative Directors:
Daniel Federman, Michael Lebowitz
URL:
http://www.sonypictures.com/
movies/identity/
ID:
04019N

Can you talk about some of the technical issues and technical objectives of the site?

Our main technical objective was to strike an optimal balance between viewing resolution, audio compression and file size. Given that NIKEBasketball.com tends to attract young and Web savvy users, supported by hi-bandwidth connections, we had some leeway as far as file size. But nonetheless, finding the right balance was also our greatest technical challenge and concern. In the end we arrived at the appropriate mix of performance and quality with the help of an intuitive Flash video player that identifies user's connection speeds and thorough audio/video compression testing.

What was the inspiration behind the art direction of the site?

The inspiration for Hooptown came from street art. First we made a mural of our hero's story. Then we entered into the world of that mural, animating the grafitti and bringing the story to life. We went to actual courts and shot the walls surrounding them and placed the entire animation onto these courts. We were after a new storytelling model based on the language of the streets—urban, animated hieroglyphics.

Art Director:
Nathan Iverson
Writer:
Jason Marks
Programmers:
Charles Duncan, Alan Ho
Producers:
Winston Binch, Shawn Natko
Designers:
Andrew Hsu, David Morrow
Information Architect:
Matt Walsh
URL:
http://www.nikebasketball.com
ID:
04020N

ONE INTERACTIVE CD-ROM TO RULE THEM ALL

Was the creative team intimidated by working on such an epic project surrounded by huge media attention and with a critical, diehard fanbase?

Not at all. In fact we were extremely motivated and enthusiastic about the opportunity as it allowed our creative team to design and animate around a brand that already is noted for its visually stimulating elements. So once we were given the opportunity we took it and did what we do best: create something never seen or done before which will linger in the minds of all viewers. The Blitz creative and marketing teams have been working with major brands like this for almost a decade now. With each new brand comes its boundaries and limitations as well as the freedom to expand our visual and emotional connective capabilities.

How did you manage to capture the spirit of the film in the interactive elements of the CD-ROM?

We captured it by utilizing a healthy mix of sound design and FX, music composition from the film and the Ring as the main metaphor and source of navigation throughout the CD. Additionally, we cut together behind the scenes content to showcase how the look of the film was derived. All of these elements combined together create a cohesive and consistent look and feel with the brand while displaying content in a unique format.

Art Director:
Robert Gale
Photographer/Illustrator:
Tim Pixton
Programmer:
Lucas Meijer
Agency Producers:
Ivan Todorov, Gregg Apirian
Creative Director:
Ken Martin
ID:
04051N

AGENCY Blitz Digital Studios/North Hollywood
client New Line Cinema/Sponsored by Dell

How did the client respond to the work?
How did users respond?

New Line Cinema was blown away with the end product. They hired us specifically because they knew we'd deliver a product beyond what other companies would normally deliver, but they definitely received more than they were expecting. In addition, the CD's sponsor, DELL, was also extremely pleased with the outcome of the CD.

A SALES TOOL FOR THE DIGITAL ERA

Like Porsche's advanced driving capabilities, Carmichael Lynch set out to create a sales and promotional tool that would combine technological innovation and superior style.

In what capacity was this CD-ROM used as a sales tool?
It was given to salespeople. They could let a customer interact with some of the features to learn more about the Cayenne while waiting for a test drive. (Vehicles were limited at launch.) There were also features like a screen saver that salespeople could download to run on their screens in the dealership or pass on to customers via e-mail as a means of encouraging a visit to the dealer.

What technical steps did the team take to make the CD-ROM interactivity reflect the Porsche brand?
The look and the interface were inspired by the Cayenne microsite. Porsche is all about high performance. This meant we had to be sure that the CD worked quickly and reliably. We also wanted to make it as non-intrusive as possible so we designed it to open and operate in a controlled window rather than taking over the whole screen. That way the salesperson could keep it up and running without having to close out of it to do other work. Like Porsche's advanced driver-aids, we wanted the interface to be as unobtrusive as possible and make sure the salesperson didn't feel as if they were losing control of their machine every time they booted up.

Writer:
Glen Fellman
Programmer:
Shannon Jackson
Designer:
T. Scott Major
ID:
04021N

Agency Carmichael Lynch/Minneapolis
client Porsche Cars North America

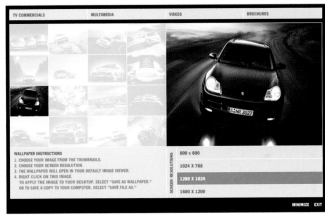

A CINEMATIC MEANS TO VISUALIZING CITY THEORY

Discuss some of the technical issues of the execution. What software was used in the production?

A gyro loaded camera ACE-601 and a digital hard disc enables maximum seventy-two-fold magnification with hardly any wobble, which you can see from the film. Yet, only the quick decision-making of our shooting crew has made this film possible. Digital technology, I must say, can only be efficient when it meets analog skill.

What was the client's brief? Describe some specific executions of elements of the brief.

"Tokyo Scanner" was originally created for The Global City exhibition, held in spring 2004 to commemorate the opening of Roppongi Hills, one of the largest redevelopment projects in Japan. The client, Mori Building Co., as well as the developer of Roppongi Hills, requested us to visualize city theory. At the first meeting, producer Mr. Yabe gave us his idea that shooting Tokyo from the sky can describe the city itself easily, but it should also be very unique. He wanted the city to be "scanned." As soon as this idea came up, I knew exactly what to do technically and decided to develop it by using techniques I had long used since my former commercial film work. By combining zooming in and out with high-powered objective, the audience can immediately understand this huge urbanized city from the macro view while still sensing its intimacy from the close-ups. I thought this was "how to scan a city."

Who was sent the CD-ROM and how did the users respond?

Retailed to Public at the Museum shop Art and Design Store in Roppongi hills.

Art Director:
Mamoru Oshii
Writer:
Mamoru Oshii
Programmer:
Masaji Shiina
Production Company:
Digital Frontier
Producer:
Toshio Yabe
Designer:
Noriyoshi Kawahara
Information Architect:
Hiroaki Matsu
Creative Director:
Hiroaki Matsu
ID:
04022N

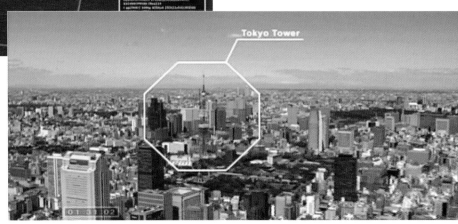

POCKETING INNOVATION ON A USB MEMORY UNIT

This is a really innovative piece. Can you talk about the design and development of the Pocket hard drive?

Since there was so much new and interesting information to share about the RX 330, and we were looking to utilize the "Putting the World on Notice" print and television campaign that was breaking at the time, a CD-ROM would have been helpful to deliver the wealth of content that was required. We were looking to include elements such as video from the television spots, interactive elements, images and product details.

However, since we wanted to point out how technologically advanced the RX 330 was, we needed a medium that was also a technological leap, which hardly describes a CD-ROM. The solution: We paired an enticing direct mail piece with an actual 16MB USB Memory Drive that activated when inserted into a computer's USB port, and delivered video content from the "Putting the World on Notice" television spot entitled "Boardroom," and then seamlessly transitioned to an interactive dossier Flash piece with rich content. The solution was not only a first for Lexus and TeamOne, but the first time anyone had used a USB Memory Unit in advertising.

What was the client's brief?

When Lexus was ready to launch their new RX 330 Luxury Utility Vehicle, they wanted to send a comprehensive direct mail piece to some very qualified leads. To begin with, we put together an e-mail campaign to bring in and qualify leads. They wanted to target those leads by leveraging the "Putting the World on Notice" print and television campaign that was running at the time.

Art Directors:
Ede Schwiezer, James Hendry
Writers:
Bill Day, Craig Crawford
Programmer:
WDDG
Digital Artist/Multimedia:
WDDG
Agency Producers:
Andrew Rosen, Susanna Leighton
Designer:
WDDG
Creative Directors:
Gabrielle Mayeur, Jon Pearce,
James Dalthorp
ID:
04023N

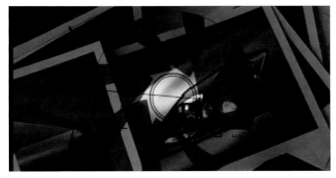

USING DIGITAL MEDIA THAT'S NOT FOR THE BIRDS

To challenge the perception that the Ford Sportka was a "girls" car, Ogilvy & Mather targeted the young male audience and launched this whimsical viral campaign that soon became an Internet phenomenon.

Art Directors:
Rob Messeter, Mike Crowe
Writers:
Mike Crowe, Rob Messeter
Creative Directors:
Malcolm Poynton, James Sinclair
URL:
www.creative-awards.co.uk/fordka
ID:
04024N

What was the client's brief?
By launching Sportka, an aggressively-styled version of the Ka with a sportier engine, Ford aimed to broaden the appeal to young men. The brief was to launch Sportka in the UK, and thus target a new young male audience who thought of the Ka as more feminine and wouldn't be caught dead driving one.

What were the solutions to achieving the brief?
"Sportka. The Ka's Evil Twin," was developed as a communications idea by Ogilvy. This challenged the perception of Ka as a girl's car. Black humor was used to dramatise the strategy and a viral medium to convey the message. The viral showed a pigeon being batted out of the air by the Sportka. Humor made the viral forwardable, meaning that communications were received by young men from their friends, rather than directly from Ford. Thus the endorsement came from a trusted and respected source. The Web address meant the target was actively passing on communications about Sportka to each other.

How successful was this project?
The total number of viral downloads from independent Web sites is untraceable. However, there were 213,413 downloads from the Evil Twin Web site alone. In total, there were 615,214 hits on the site with 378,823 unique visitors. The efficient, low-budget campaign generated valuable PR coverage and awareness, and was even featured on TV shows as far away as Australia. Sales to date are nearly 3,000 units, 68% of which are high-end SE models.

www.the-eviltwin.co.uk

VISIONS FROM THE FUTURE OF MOBILE BROADBAND

Vodafone provides a cutting-edge look into the future of mobile broadband technology with a visually stunning Web site that pushes the boundaries of multimedia design.

Art Director:
Robert Lindström
Writers:
Gabriele Dangel, David Eriksson, Alan Richardson
Photographer/Illustrator:
Hakan Moberg
Programmers:
Martin Klasson, PM Nordqvist
Producers:
Roger Stighäll, Alan Richardson
Designer:
Charlotta Lundqvist
URL:
http://www.vodafone.com/futurevision
ID:
04026N

Also Awarded
Gold:
Beyond the Banner – Single
04011N

How did the idea for the Future Vision campaign come about? What was the objective of the campaign?
After all the press coverage about 3G, people wanted to know: What can we actually do with mobile broadband? Where are the benefits? Where will telecommunication take us in 7 to 10 years? People asked Vodafone, the industry leader, for the answer.

Talk about the technical execution. The campaign was oriented around future technologies. How important was it that the site reflects the most impressive design and interactivity?
The future site is all about showing and exploring how future technology can possibly be experienced. Therefore, it felt like a natural step to also work on a new solution for design, interactivity and navigation that had not been seen before. Our final solution was developed around what photo technique to use and how to use 3-D and film most efficiently. We also went through multiple usability tests to confirm that the user understood our interactive solution. Along the road we faced many challenges when building this site. The production was aimed at broadband users, but we still had to deliver small file sizes for smoothness. Therefore, the video-compression was important. Streaming and preloading "behind-the-scenes" was also essential to make the exploration of the site quick and responsive to the user.

AGENCY Vodafone/Newbury
CLIENT Vodafone Group Services

How have users responded?

The reaction was amazing. Just one day after the launch the number of visitors to the Vodafone corporate site went up by 30 percent. Twenty-thousand visitors came to the site on a daily rate.

Even more impressive were their comments. For example: "This is a truly amazing Web site, the best I have ever seen! As a student studying Industrial Design at CCS in Detroit, it is important for me and students like me to understand and be up to date with new and innovative technologies. Seeing the possibilities that are in the near future is very inspirational because it is these types of technological advancements that will shape my future as a designer. If we become better connected then it will definitely be a step towards making the world a better place."

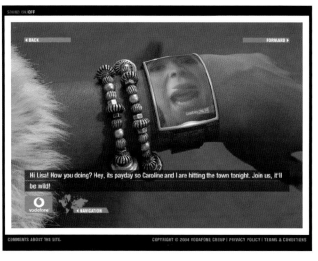

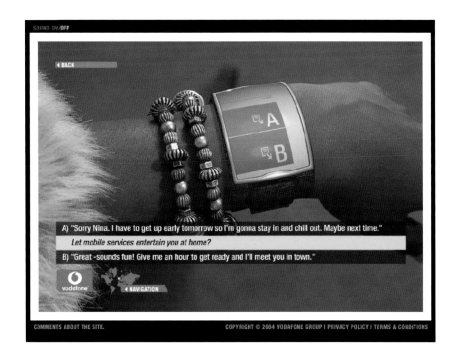

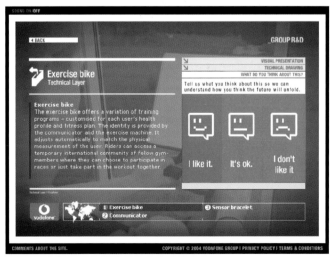

agency Vodafone/Newbury
client Vodafone Group Services

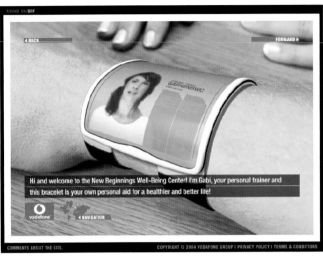

THE INSIDE STORY OF VOLVO'S INSIDE STORY

The creative team at Forsman & Bodenfors set out to make the Volvo S40 Inside Story site more like a movie than a Web site and in the process covered the many angles of innovation.

Art Directors:
Martin Cedergren, Anders Eklind, Andreas Malm, Mikko Timonen
Writers:
Filip Nilsson, Jacob Nelson
Photographer/Illustrator:
Peter Gehrke
Programmer:
Koko Kaka Entertainment
Agency Producer:
Mathias Appelblad
Producer:
Mathias Appelblad
Designer:
Lars Johansson
URL:
http://demo.fb.se/e/s40
ID:
04027N

Discuss the technical requirements/challenges of the execution, specifically the seamless 360-degree camera rotation.

When we set out to make the Volvo S40 The Inside Story site, we really tried to challenge what had been done before on the Internet. Our goal was to create a site that communicated more like a movie. Using our experience from making TV commercials, we created an interactive way to present the communicative concept. One of the most challenging tasks was to demonstrate the new Volvo S40 both from the inside and outside. We had seen plenty of 3-D and QTVR rotations of cars before, but none that could fit the communicative and visual concept of the campaign. Therefore we decided to make it in a totally new way—instead of moving the car, we moved the user. From over 200 images, taken by one of Sweden's eminent fashion photographers, we created a seamless presentation of exterior and interior of the car. We made no compromises whatsoever on the quality of the images and the softness of the motions in the animations. It was pretty hard work, but in the end, we did it.

AGENCY Forsman & Bodenfors/Gothenburg
CLIENT Volvo Cars Sweden/Volvo S40

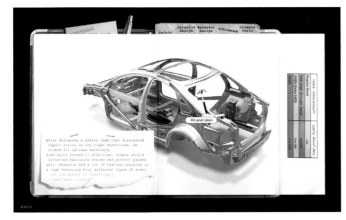

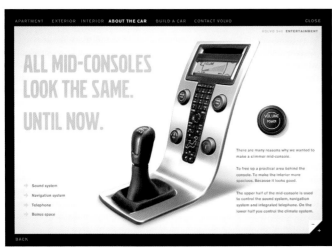

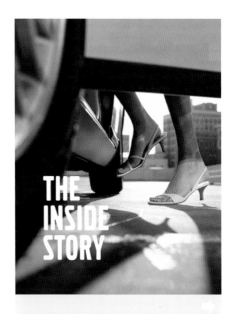

Talk about the client's brief and how you successfully implemented it.

The client wanted the Web part of the campaign to fully expose the car from every angle. As the TV ads only were focused from the inside of the car, the Web was expected to be used as the ultimate tool to really dig deep into the car; features, design and safety. As the launch campaign was highly targeted for a younger group, we were asked to fulfill the need of delivering on the "fashion aspect" of the vehicle. Urban, designer, young, lifestyle oriented—all these were important elements of the brief.

EXECUTING AN IMMERSIVE SPEED EXPERIENCE

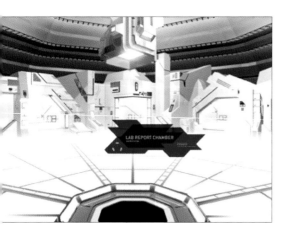

Art Directors:
Rei Inamoto, Jerome Austria
Writer:
Jason Marks
Programmers:
Raymond Vazquez, Lucas Shuman,
Martin Legowiecki, Chuck Genco,
Stan Weichers, Hamid Younessi,
Scott Prindle
Producer:
Jennifer Allen
Designers:
Jerome Austria, Mikhail Gervits,
Hiroko Ishimura, Gui Borchert
Information Architect:
Carlos Gomez de Ilarena
URL:
www.nikelab.com
ID:
04028N

R/GA does a lot of work for Nike.
How does the creative team keep themselves fresh?
What are some design/interactivity inspirations?
One thing that we do that might differ from other projects is that we include the entire team in the creative process, not just the creatives but everyone involved in the production of the site. For example, programmers often bring interesting technical innovations or ways to solve problems. Everyone on the team is encouraged to look for inspiration all around them. It is important, however, to stay on top of what's happening digitally so that we can avoid doing things that have already been done.

Talk about the client's brief for Nike Lab.
How did it differ from other Nike site design briefs?
The brief for Nikelab is infamous for it's basic requirement: make the coolest site ever. It has now become a running joke (although Nike is still quite serious about the requirement), especially since we must continually strive to top ourselves. How do you go beyond the coolest site ever? Another interesting distinction between the Nike Lab brief and other Nike briefs is the location of our target audience. While most Nike sites are focused on a particular sport such as running or basketball, the target audience for Nike Lab is horizontally located across various sports, music, film and fashion.

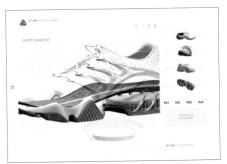

What are some of the elements of the site that required more time and effort with regard to programming and design?

An interesting challenge for concept, design and programming was to portray the idea of "speed"—ironically, to experience actual speed on a Web site would be to experience nothing, since everything would be immediate. We had to figure out a way to create space or distance that users could travel through in order to have an immersive "speed experience." Because of that, all of our concepts revolved around 3-D space. But actual 3-D would have been too time consuming and heavy, so we had to conceive of clever design and programming executions that would mimic 3-D, but be much less production-heavy and faster to load.

THE TECHNICAL CHALLENGE OF CREATING A UNIVERSE

Informing visitors of the elegance of Volkswagen's most luxurious large car was no easy task for London's Tribal DDB. Yet after 4 months, a new online star was born.

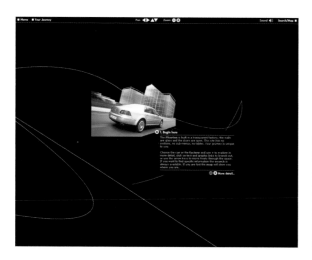
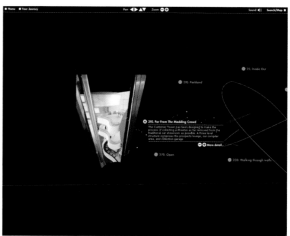

Art Directors:
Tim Vance, Dave Bedwood, Sam Ball, Robin Garms
Writer:
Robin Garms
Programmers:
Chris Jenkins, Dave Cox, Nicole Scholeter
Producer:
Sally Gallagher
Designer:
Tim Vance
Information Architect:
Chris Jenkins
Creative Directors:
Sam Ball, Dave Bedwood
URL:
www.thephaeton.co.uk
ID:
04029N

What was the objective of the site?
Discuss the client's brief.

To convince people that Volkswagen, the people's car manufacturer, could build a luxury sedan.

In the UK, luxury car buyers look for heritage and prestige. The market s dominated by Mercedes Benz, BMW and Jaguar. Newer brands such as Lexus struggle, despite their evident quality. VW is most famous for its Beetle and Golf—family cars for everyone. It has never built anything bigger or more expensive than a Passat. The site had to both persuade visitors that Volkswagen had the knowledge and skill to build a truly amazing big car, and that the VW badge could be associated with luxury, style and elegance.

The art direction is very distinct.
What were some influences and inspirations behind the look and interactivity of the site?

A typical approach to showcasing a car on automotive Web sites is to provide a 360-degree internal view. This is meant to show off some of the car's attributes and create a feel for the ambience inside the vehicle. In fact it makes large luxury cars seem small and claustrophobic. Tribal's creatives wanted to get as far away from that as possible, and so the idea emerged for a car that had been exploded so that every single element could be examined from any angle. For a car of the ingenuity and complexity of the Phaeton, this appeared to be a way of allowing users to choose the areas and the depth to which they wanted to explore.

AGENCY Tribal DDB/London
CLIENT Volkswagen

Modeling every single component would have been an epic task, and would perhaps not have created the feeling of peace, serenity and space that the Phaeton seemed to exude. So each component—in fact, each "product story"—within the Phaeton became a single point, and the environment became a simple space that contained these points: The "Phaeton Universe."

What were some of the technical challenges?
The whole project was a technical challenge for the team, who were working in Flash 6 soon after its first release. (This was essential to deliver the video clips.) Tribal's main Flash programmer started from scratch three times as new and better ways of making the site work became apparent. Typically, sites that work in 3-D are difficult to find your way around, as the user has to follow the programmer's preferred method of navigation. The beauty of the Phaeton site is that the user is completely free to move in or out or around the universe, to use hyperlinks or the back and forward controls of the browser to explore. Usability research proved that this had been worthwhile—different people do indeed use different approaches.

In the end the project took over four months. The full code, when printed out in 7-point script, covers 56 pages. The final site is almost infinitely flexible—new "stars" can be added at any time, galaxies of product information can be made more or less central. But Volkswagen, who are completely enamored with it, haven't wanted to change a thing.

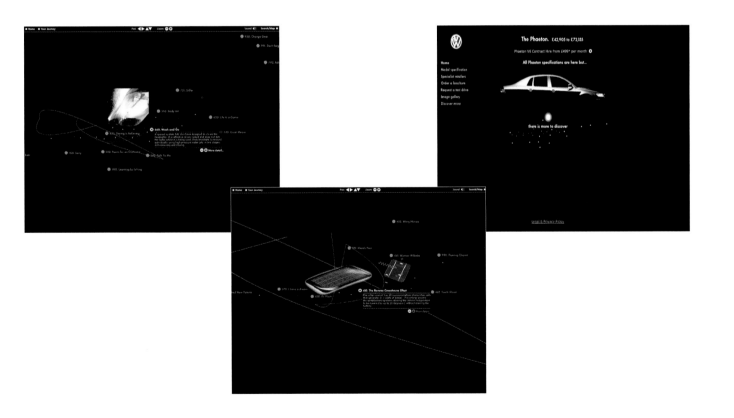

AN EXERCISE IN TIMELESS INDUSTRIAL DESIGN

The site incorporates a lot of multimedia elements. Discuss the technical requirements/challenges of the execution.
When we approached the Chrysler Crossfire Experience CD-ROM project we immediately realized that audiences most likely haven't seen a single shot of this sexy vehicle. Maybe they've caught a glimpse of the side grill, but the odds of them really seeing this contemporary roadster in action were slim to none. Based on this, we wanted to incorporate as many video components as possible, particularly in our main navigation. For the four main sections of the CD-ROM we created 30-second looping videos of the vehicle in various environments (on the road, in a 360-degree spin etc.). This enabled us to provide audiences with an instant read on the vehicle simply by rolling over the navigation.

Given that we were working in a CD-ROM environment, the technical requirements were not as strict as they are for the design and development of a Web site. CD-ROMs enable us to push our creative ideas that much further and we're able to dive into a project knowing that we don't have to be too cautious of file size constraints or screen resolutions. We're able to utilize every pixel on an 800 x 600 screen and we don't have to worry about compression or creating "simulated" video. With the CD-ROM environment we're able to explore the integration of video within our overall interface, which is something we'd love to be able to do on the Web, but the bandwidth is just not there yet.

Programmers:
Shea Gonyo, Gicheol Lee
Production Company:
Firstborn Multimedia
Producer:
Jeremy Berg
Designer:
Vas Sloutchevsky
Information Architect:
Vas Sloutchevsky
Creative Director:
Vas Sloutchevsky
ID:
04030N

agency Firstborn Multimedia/New York
client BBDO/The Arnell Group

Talk a little about the client's brief and how you successfully implemented it.

The purpose of the project was to expose audiences to the Chrysler Crossfire in the most engaging and exciting way possible. We needed to convey in a visual way that this vehicle was the first drivable result of the merger of Daimler-Benz and the Chrysler Corporation. The Chrysler Crossfire was designed and engineered with equal measures of American imagination and German precision. Based on that, the overall experience had to be elegant, demonstrate technical prowess and provide creative ways to explore all of the exciting nuances of the vehicle.

Once we began working with all of the rich photography that the Arnell Group supplied us with, we just knew we'd be able to create an effective sales and marketing tool that would get everyone truly excited about this unique roadster. We immediately knew that we wanted to create unique ways for users to explore every inch of the vehicle. For the exterior and interior photos, we provided the audience with a long horizontal strip comprised of roughly a dozen photos each. Users could easily pan the strip left and right to find a photo and click on any image to access a pristine 800 x 600 enlarged view.

When it came to creating the color selector section, we determined that we wanted the audience to do as little clicking as possible. Each color and interior option, as well as a "background environment shot" (e.g. city road, highway, etc.), is accessed via simple mouse rollovers. For the most part, the only clicking that is done in this section is to see the vehicle from different angles.

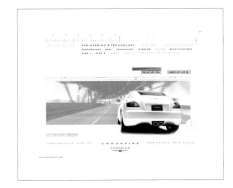

We tried to present the car as the most desirable and prestigious object of industrial design. The black and white approach creates the sense of luxury and timelessness, while the interactive aspect of the experience reveals hints about the sophisticated nature of the vehicle.

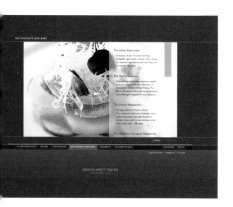

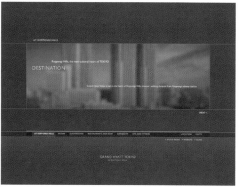

Art Director:
Shinzo Fukui
Programmer:
Eiji Muroichi
Producer:
Maiko Hotta
Designer:
Eiji Muroichi
Creative Director:
Shinzo Fukui
ID:
04031N

What was the most important element of the execution of the client's brief?

The Grand Hyatt Tokyo has a unique personality—it meets the challenges of this age while being rich in innovative dynamism. When the concept was outlined to us, we first set up a site for pre-opening use, which allowed us to gain a full understanding of the appeal of the hotel. However, we found it quite difficult when we came to produce the hotel tour CD-ROM. This was because we had almost no materials with which to fully express how great the hotel really was. The most important thing for us to do was to select which of the available items to "show" and "tell." We decided that, rather than create a tour of the physical interior of the hotel, we would show how the hotel's functionality works in partnership with its concepts. Many hotel tour CD-ROMs are all about showing as much of the completed interior as they can. They use a lot of 3-D animation and other high-tech tricks, but they can never duplicate the actual experience of being in the hotel.

Agency Business Architects/Tokyo
client Mori Hospitality Corporation

The CD-ROM takes the idea of an e-brochure quite literally. Describe the technical process of converting a print brochure into a dynamic e-brochure.

While the CD-ROM was inspired and informed by some of the conventions of a paper brochure, our design was anything but a literal adaptation.

We started by dreaming a little. We thought, what if you could take a paper brochure and do anything with it? What if you tossed aside the restrictions of paper and could let people reach into the brochure and spin the car and play with features? What if when you turned a page and saw the convertible against beautiful rolling hills, you could actually see the mist move across the scene and hear the birds singing? We wanted to bring people as close to the car as possible.

The e-booklet came out of all of these thoughts. In essence, we married the best of a brochure to the best of the Web. Working with Macromedia Director with Flash overlays and embedded video, the team was able to bring the dream to life. The result is the e-booklet that sits on your computer's desktop. In creating it, we played with the notion of paper, and created an experience that is at once familiar (turning the pages of a brochure), but that also surprises and delights.

Art Director:
Joe Sharrino
Writers:
Melissa Wyer, Sheri Kaufmann
Designer:
Barry Nolan
Creative Director:
Sheri Kaufmann
ID:
04032N

A NEW TIMELINE FOR FLEXIBLE MOVIE STREAMING

To provide a dynamic and interactive Web site for Acht Frankfurt Digital Solutions, Germany's Scholz & Volkmer created a streamlined method to view a complete reel without a click.

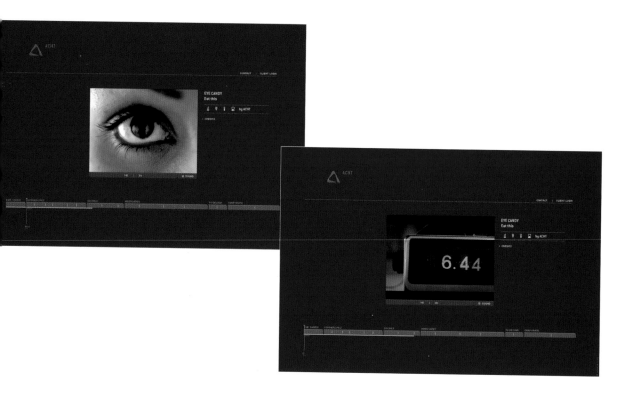

What were some of the technical innovations used in the site production?

For this site Scholz & Volkmer developed a new streaming facility (loader management) that makes it possible for the user to view the Web site, i.e. the complete show reel without a click, just like a video cassette/DVD. The user navigates with a new type of timeline navigation (magnifier function) making it possible to directly switch to categories, individual spots and frames. Through the CMS, Acht-Frankfurt can at any time independently reconfigure the content of the show reel by including and excluding new spots. It thus serves as a portfolio that is always up-to-date.

How did you execute the client's brief?

The brief was as simple as the solution: Conception and realization of the Internet and Extranet (client login) appearance for the recently founded digital postproduction company Acht-Frankfurt.

What was the objective of the site?

To provide a "dynamic and interactive show reel" showing an exclusive work selection realized by Acht-Frankfurt. The combination of the linearity of a movie and the non-linearity of the Internet media has been the main challenge in this application.

Programmers:
Duc-Thuan Bui, Manfred Kraft
Designers:
Heike Brockmann, Jenny Fitz
Creative Director:
Heike Brockmann
URL:
www.acht-frankfurt.de
ID:
04033N

AGENCY Scholz & Volkmer/Wiesbaden
CLIENT Acht Frankfurt Digital Solutions

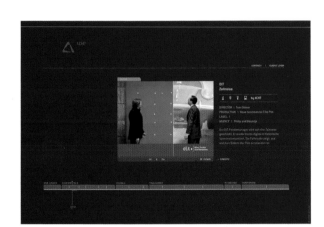

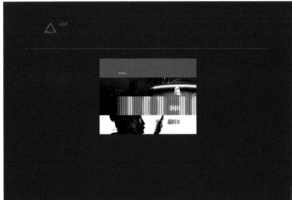

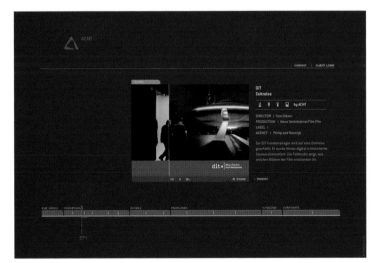

AN ONLINE PORTFOLIO GETS THE PICTURE

Photographer Jimmy McGrath had Juxt Interactive construct a highly creative online portfolio of his work. Sometimes a picture is worth much more than one thousand words.

Discuss some of the technical issues of the execution?
A few elements of the project turned out to be bigger obstacles than we planned, and the Actionscript was not one of them. The hardest aspect to accomplish was creating a seamless flow between Jimmy's photography and the custom illustration. Lining up the two images was a tedious, difficult process. Also, the volume of assets was a challenge, both from a production standpoint, and coming up with unique, engaging illustrations for every photograph.

Talk about the client's brief and willingness to explore the graphic overlays over the photographs.
Jimmy is a fashion and celebrity photographer based in Los Angeles, who happened to go to college with our CMO, Josh Mooney. Jimmy came to Juxt seeking to create a Web presence that propelled his work and his name above the daily barrage of postcards and portfolios sent to ad agency creative directors. He walked into our offices with only his portfolio and a request for something super creative. He trusted Todd and the Juxt team to create a brand, and to connect with the hearts and minds of decision makers looking to hire a guy that can "get the shot," something Jimmy prides himself on being able to do.

Art Director:
Todd Purgason
Producers:
Steve Wages, Jason Deal
Designers:
Luis Sanz, Paul Drohan, Nate Smith, Mike Hansen, Anthony Furlong, Shant Parsechian
Creative Director:
Todd Purgason
URL:
www.jimmymcgrathphoto.com
ID:
04034N

AGENCY Juxt Interactive/Newport Beach
CLIENT Jimmy McGrath

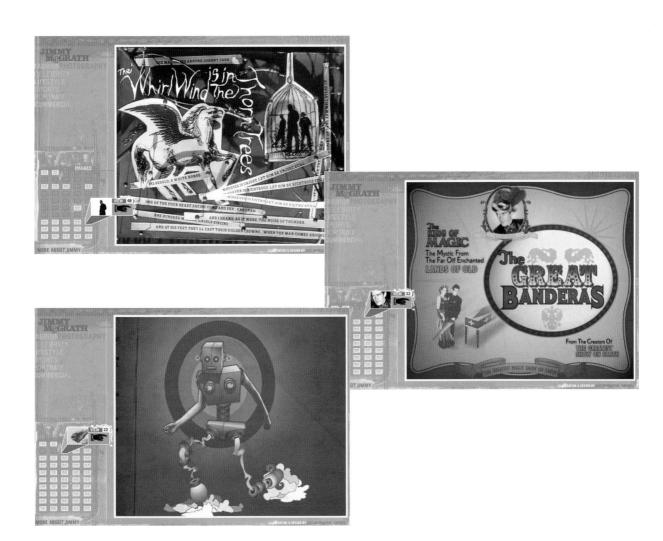

What has the response been like from users?

The site has generated international interest in Jimmy's work. The site has had literally zero marketing outside of the design community and the URL on Jimmy's business card. Word of mouth has created a ton of traffic, and requests to include images from the site in books have come from Germany and elsewhere. Has the site impacted Jimmy's business? The client cannot pinpoint a gig he landed strictly from someone seeing his site. But when he refers prospective clients to the site, they gain confidence that he can deliver. And that has been extremely valuable to his business.

A STORIED TRADITION MEETS THE DIGITAL AGE

J. Walter Thompson and connect@jwt combine talents to deliver an organic, media-rich interactive CD-ROM recruiting tool for the United States Marine Corps.

Art Directors:
Isobel Moutrey, Todd Zerger
Writers:
Jeff Thompson, Nicole Duclos
Photographers/Illustrators:
Jason Maris, Nigel Marson, Filewurx, Slingshot Studios
Programmers:
Marc Bloomquist, Stacey Roelofs
Digital Artists/Multimedia:
Outback Editorial, Atomic Dog
Producers:
Angie Trewhitt, George Medland, Buffy Torres
Designer:
Marc Bloomquist
Information Architects:
Elena Murray, Bryan Perry
Creative Directors:
Alan Whitley, Scott Nelson
ID:
04035N

Discuss some of the technical issues of the execution?
This project came with high expectations from the Marine Corps and represented one of the most intense collaborations to date between JWT Atlanta's traditional creative department and digital@jwt (now connect@jwt). We had art directors and writers from both sides trying to interpret direction. And we put a lot of pressure on ourselves, because we wanted to exceed the interactive capability of competitive and past CD-ROM products. We had a big, complex brand story to tell, and this seemed like the place to tell it. We wanted it to feel seamless with the rest of the brand communication, so we needed to infuse pieces of traditional communication like television and print onto a digital medium. This presented some real issues when it came to production, because the digital world is so different from the analog one.

The other difficulty was the feeling of flying blind in trying to create an accurate model for what we were about to do. With print and television projects, we always create prototypes of the intended piece at a fairly early stage in the process. With this project, to create a true prototype would have amounted to nearly complete programming, which is expensive and time consuming. So initial development relied a lot on leaps of faith by all the team members and the client. It wasn't until the late stages of production that everyone could really see where we were going.

What was the client's brief?

What are some of the specific implementations of the brief?

We knew we'd be trying to push the technical edge of what CD-ROMs could do; we just didn't know where that edge was. So the brief pertained more to the intended use. The Marines needed recruiters to be able to give this piece away at will, with no introduction or setup, and have it motivate a kid to go to Marines.com to find out more. They wanted it to be highly informative and fun to play with. They wanted a piece the kid could use to get to know the Corps, with no pressure. It turned out to be the best brief, because we had a great deal of freedom to create something unexpected. And I think we did. The piece has a huge Flash animation intro, eight custom edited videos the user can watch, 14 interactive content areas and seven custom downloads. It's pretty fun to interact with.

Our favorite features: We wanted to have a certain portion of the CD-ROM be a mandatory ride, in order to communicate the overall brand message thoroughly. But after that, we wanted the user to be able to explore freely. Finally, we wanted the option of whether or not to jump to Marines.com to belong to the user. We ended up creating a cool 2-minute Flash animation that featured videos and even elements from Marine Corps TV spots embedded within the Flash movie. That was difficult to pull off, because we had to build the 13 or so video features first, then build the Flash movie around them. The hardest part was creating the intricate music track that drove the movie. We'd create music, and then create animation for it. The animation would seem too long, so we'd shorten the track. Then, we'd go back and do it all again. That was painful, but worth it. In the end, the feel of the animation was very fluid as it moved from video feature to video feature. We were also very proud of the music track, because we created it mostly using actual sounds from the Marine Corps environment. We'd take the sound of Marines dumping over the side of a Zodiac into the water, or drill team rifles, and create musical rhythm out of them. We carried those rhythms all the way through the piece. It's very organic.

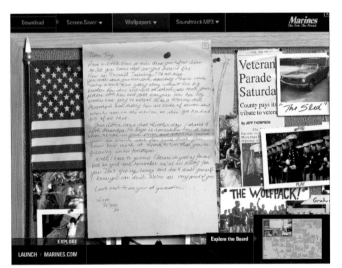

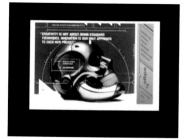

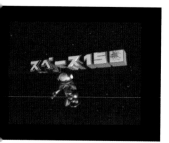

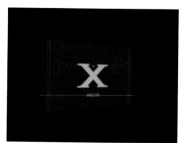

Art Director:
Jason Strong
Writers:
Billy Jurewicz, Dan McNeill
Photographer/Illustrator:
Dan McNeill
Programmers:
Steve Stwalley, Marc Jensen,
Ryan Senechal, Jason Prieve
Digital Artists/Multimedia:
Steve Stwalley, Dan McNeill
Agency Producer:
Rebecca Longawa
Producers:
Lindsay Wenner, Tirzah Larson
Designers:
Jason Strong, Todd Bartz
Information Architect:
Todd Bartz
Director:
Billy Jurewicz
Creative Director:
Billy Jurewicz
ID:
04036N

What was the objective of the CD-ROM?
The objective was to celebrate the evolutionary story of space
150's unique version upgrade. Just as software advances from version to
version, space150 embraces this concept by upgrading its very own Web site,
business cards and identity every 150 days. Proving to its clients that one
must over-commit to evolving technology to stay proactive in the digital war.

Describe the technical process and execution.
Utilizing past and current examples of space150's work, a script was written
to embrace the version 1-10 timeline. The voiceover was recorded and laid in
Final Cut Pro, where all the elements were assembled. Later the movie was
converted and streamed live on the space150 site using Flash 6 technology.

**Has this been a successful self-promotional tool
for space150?**
Extremely successful. Today, our v10 is the most popular and most viewed
section of our site. A demand for a new version site is well on its way.

agency space150/Minneapolis
client space150

How did the creative team come up with such an interesting idea?

We wanted to change perceptions about a credible but unsexy brand. We chose an e-mail and Internet approach after being challenged with the task of communicating to a small, computer savvy target audience of agency producers and creatives who have no time along with a number of music industry producers and A&R people.

The agency created five e-mail letters that linked to both a "decoded" version of the letter displaying hidden alien messages and to five streamed mpeg mini-commercials. The letters were delivered as GIFs and appear to be hand written—sort of low-tech meets the Web. They appear to come from moonshine-addled, wacky-tobaccey- puffin' southerners who have had dubious experiences with aliens.

The letters show the author's deteriorating mental state while describing outrageous, incredible experiences of alien intervention. They provided two links: one to a decoded version of the letter and another to a streamed 30-second mpeg commercial.

How did the client respond to the work?
How did users respond?

The client loved it. Users noticed. Site traffic increased from zero to 6 GB a day in the middle of the campaign, and business had picked up considerably after the campaign had run it's course.

Art Directors:
Adrian McNamara, Albert Jangtong
Writer:
Gaby Bush
Agency Producer:
Brendon Everett
Production Company:
Showpage
Producer:
Steve Lloyd
Creative Directors:
Gaby Bush, Richard Mirabelli
URL:
www.bushatkins.com.au/tiger
ID:
04037N

ENHANCING THE ONLINE SHOPPING EXPERIENCE

Art Director:
Yzabelle Munson
Writer:
Kristina Grish
Programmers:
Raymond Vazquez, David Morrow,
Christine Reindl
Producer:
Afua Brown
Designers:
Johanna Langford, Jeannie Kang
Information Architect:
Erin Lynch
URL:
http://www.nikegoddess.com
ID:
04038N

**Can you talk about some of the technical issues
and technical objectives of the site?**
We used Flash to make the site more dynamic and to make the transition
from content to shopping nearly seamless for the user. Flash has a reputation
for large downloads. We had to be vigilant about optimizing images and
using smart code to keep file sizes reasonable.

**What are some important considerations when designing
a site modeled for e-commerce?**
Unlike a brick and mortar shop, your digital consumer cannot touch or try
on the product. We attempted to compensate for this by offering superior
product display. Our shots were larger than average. We allowed users
to rotate the product to see a front and back view. We also called out
product details such as pockets, mesh and texture in pop-up close-ups
of the features.

AGENCY R/GA/New York
CLIENT Nike

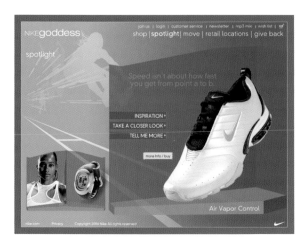

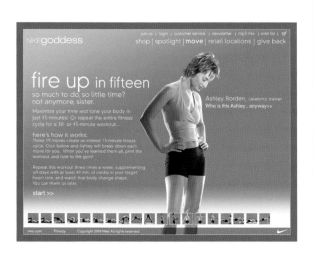

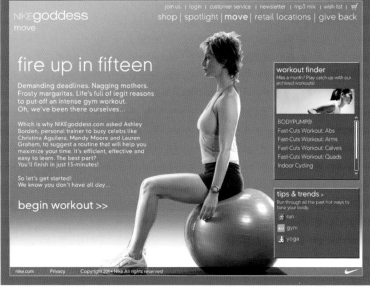

PUTTING ONE FOOT IN FRONT OF THE OTHER ONLINE

SKIP INTRO

nike.com | nikeid - europe

Describe the creative process and technical challenges faced by the team.

The prime objective of this site was to make it easy to create and order your own shoes as well as look great. This meant the process required equal parts functionality and creativity. Once the usability was in place and the processes mapped out, we set to work making it look and sound just right.

Simple and elegant Flash combined with product-focused design makes the process of making and ordering shoes not just a number of clicks, but also an inspiring and rewarding experience. Who says e-commerce and branding should be mutually exclusive?

Talk about the client's brief and discuss your success in translating the client's ideas.

The brief was to build a site that would let users design, tag and order their own personal Nike shoes. Given the popularity of the site and the number of sold products, we think we nailed it.

How did online consumers react to this site?

The online consumers have reacted the way we hoped by ordering a lot of shoes and other products.

Art Director:
Rasmus Frandsen
Writer:
Thomas Robson
Programmers:
Brian Dickens, Martin Baltzer
Producer:
Lars-Bo Heidemann
Designer:
Jesper Bolther
Information Architects:
Søren Schultz, Andreas Iversen
Creative Director:
Lars Bastholm
URL:
www.nikeid.com/europe
ID:
04039N

GENERATING TEST DRIVES THROUGH INGENUITY

To accomodate a Web site with variously sized content areas, IQ television group developed an adaptable multi-state navigation system that resized to the content being observed.

Discuss the technical requirements and challenges of the execution.

Probably the most technically challenging aspect in the development of AudiCPO.com was the fact that the site needed to accommodate several different sizes and types of content. The transition into the site was linked creatively with several different rich media ads and much of the presentation of content within the site called for flexibility in size. To accommodate this we developed an adaptable multi-state navigation system that expanded and contracted according to the current content being viewed. This allowed us to take full advantage of the browser canvas and to promote areas within the site based on user activity.

Art Director:
IQ television group
Writer:
IQ television group
Programmer:
IQ television group
Creative Director:
IQ television group
URL:
www.audicpo.com
ID:
04040N

Talk a little about the client's brief and how you successfully implemented it.

The mission given to IQ from the client for this project was simple—generate test drives. Audi's success rate for converting test drives into purchases is tremendous. Therefore, our measure of success was directly tied to the number of people the site could motivate to go out and experience an Audi for themselves.

With this in mind we developed the site around our "Directed Choice" approach. This technique limits the number of choices available to the user at any given time. Not in an attempt to limit interactivity but rather to focus attention on key areas of content. Ultimately, this directs the viewer's attention and leads toward the registration process.

USING FLASH TO GET THE MOST FROM YOUR FONTS

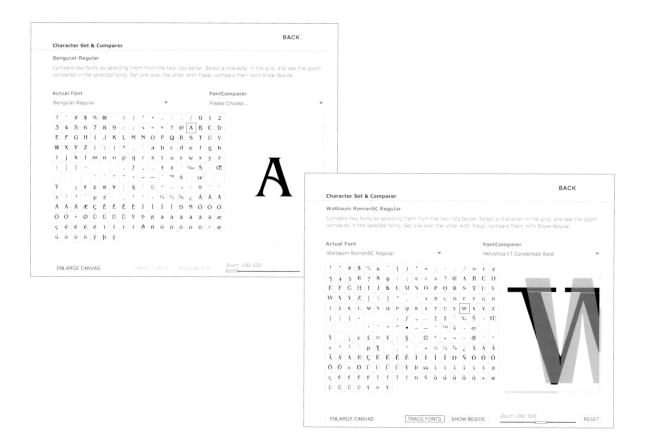

What was the objective of the site?

The Fontcomparer Tool provides enhanced information on selected fonts. The potential customer is able to compare any font in his bookmark list with each other. Even the slightest variations can be detected by showing two selected fonts side-by-side or layered one above the other. One is able to browse through the character set of the selected fonts and continuously zoom into the selected character without any loss of quality.

Can you talk about some of the technical issues and technical objectives of the site?

The Tool itself was created with Macromedia's Flash 6. The technical back-end uses OpenSource products like PHP and Ming. A script automatically converts TrueType fonts into several formats ending up in a special Shockwave Flash file, which contains the character set of each font. For the Linotype Library, over 30,000 fonts were converted.

How did users respond to the site?
How did the client respond?

All are happy.

Programmers:
Peter Reichard, Samuel Ruckstuhl, Manfred Kraft
Designer:
Elke Grober
Information Architects:
Manfred Kraft, Irmgard Weigl
Creative Director:
Michael Volkmer
URL:
www.s-v.de/projects/fontcomparer
ID:
04041N

AGENCY Scholz & Volkmer/Wiesbaden
client Linotype Library

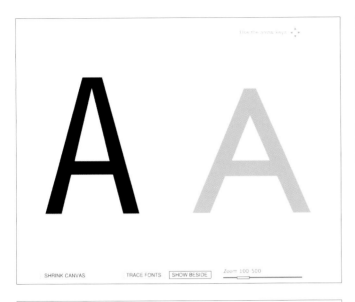

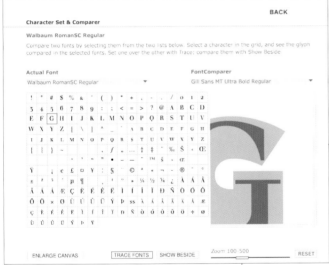

BACK

Character Set & Comparer

Walbaum RomanSC Regular

Compare two fonts by selecting them from the two lists below. Select a character in the grid, and see the glyph compared in the selected fonts. Set one over the other with Trace; compare them with Show Beside.

Actual Font   FontComparer

Walbaum RomanSC Regular   Gill Sans MT Ultra Bold Regular

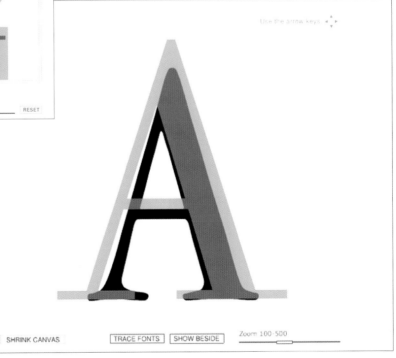

TAKING RISKS WITH GUERRILLA ONLINE TACTICS

Combining a series of non-traditional digital guerrilla marketing initiatives with more traditional advertising, Wieden + Kennedy created the phenomenon known as Beta-7.

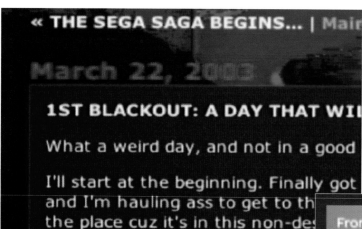

Art Director:
Robert Rasmussen
Writers:
Bobby Hershfield, Mike Monello, Ed Sanchez,
Jim Gunshanon, M. C. Johnson
Agency Producers:
Gary Krieg, Temma Shoaf
Production Company:
Chelsea Pictures
Producers:
Anthony Nelson, Chelsea Pictures
Directors:
Mike Monello, Ed Sanchez
Creative Directors:
Todd Waterbury, Ty Montague
URL:
ID:
04042N

How did the idea for the Beta-7 campaign come about? What was the objective of the campaign?

The objective of the campaign was, quite frankly, to do something different. Video game advertising essentially sticks to the same formula, relying mostly on traditional media to stimulate sales. Being a challenger brand, ESPN/ Sega wanted to take a risk and do something that the leader in the industry would never do, because the big games have so much more to lose. We also had something new to tell, a new feature, (First Person Football, which lets you play from the point of view of a player on the field), which would be the primary selling point of the game. We decided to use the Internet to speak to the hardcore gamer and use our traditional advertising not only to speak to a mass audience but also to create the façade for our conspiracy.

AGENCY Wieden + Kennedy/New York
client ESPN Videogames/Sega

The idea came about by playing into three truths: a) the game's main feature; b) the fact that a debate exists over the degree of violence in today's video games; and c) our target spends most of their day online, where they are searching out exactly what they are interested in and therefore controlling the information they take in. So we created an elaborate conspiracy theory on the Web—that this new feature would lead to random acts of violence. We knew that, on its own, this premise could be problematic, but if we expressed this as entertainment, we could promote the game in this fashion without too much controversy. This core target is willing to forgive marketing if it is entertaining or appeals to them as a respected audience. We also knew that if we could get the hardcore gamer to talk about it, others would follow. Then, by doing more traditional advertising, not only could we reach a broader audience, but the hardcore gamer might start to believe the interactive theater a bit more.

Talk about the technical execution. The campaign was oriented around a "hand-made" multimedia aesthetic. How was this done?

All we wanted was to create a debate centered on the game and provide the target with different areas to turn to, either to gain evidence or to cast doubt over whether it was real. So initially, we wanted to create some doubt. And then the goal was to convert those doubters to believers and let them carry on the debate. The way to do that was to dive so deep into the details that even the most curious would find something to make them think twice. If we printed a phone number, we set up a voicemail on that number—things like that. Authenticity was paramount. Once we casted Beta-7 and figured out his character, we were able to craft everything in such a fashion as if he had done it himself. To make flyers, he would have gone to Kinko's, laid it out in a bold font, put a rule around it and printed it out on the counter-recommended fluorescent yellow paper. To design his Web page, he would have his techie friend (a character we created named Rob) set him up a template that he could enter his blog into each day and that people could easily post to and chat at. He could contribute a share-ware font he found that replicated Sega's logo to use for the SEGA SUCKS page. This was the basic rule we followed. Whenever design and good art direction were added, they were quickly stripped away. And Beta-7 followed the same rules. He would often respond to participants' e-mails within minutes, even at three in the morning. He cursed, didn't spell-check, he drank, he just acted in character.

For the other Web sites, we simply stayed true to the character of Beta-7's Web site. Gamer Chuck was supposedly from Sega, so e-mails only came out during working hours and he was always quiet on weekends. We used legible fonts, perfect grammar, correct logos, and played-game footage for both Windows and Macintosh. A scary medical site had to post its evidence in a style that was representative of an undercover whistle-blower trying to scare people.

The characters we created dictated the look and feel of the entire campaign.

AGENCY Wieden + Kennedy/New York
CLIENT ESPN Videogames/Sega

MOTION AND MYSTERY IN A SMALL SWEDISH VILLAGE

What was the client's brief? What were the challenges?
The core objective was to raise a broad awareness for this new product launch and to provoke purchase consideration specifically within the 30-45 year old target group. While the Volvo S40's innovative features would go a long way towards moving the general perception of Volvo, the team recognized the impact of broader issues affecting general acceptance of the brand and product messages.

First, image studies had revealed that the brand perception was lagging far behind the reality of the modern Volvo ownership experience and far below levels required for conquest on a mass scale. It was imperative for the launch communication to bridge this gap.

Second, the lack of brand consideration was exacerbated by the target group's skeptical view towards advertising per se. A different communications approach was required to ensure that the launch message resonated within the target group in a meaningful way.

Third, Volvo's low share of voice versus competitors reinforced the need for a different, more radical approach. Every element of the communication needed to punch beyond its financial weight in order to cut through the clutter to create high awareness.

Fourth, the communication concept needed to accommodate a spectrum of budget levels and media mixes across European markets. Importantly, not every market was supported by TVC, so the concept needed to perform with or without this element in the communications mix.

Art Director:
Bertrand Fleuret
Writer:
Lorenzo De Rita
Agency Producer:
Tania Kane
Production Company:
MJZ
Producer:
Vincent Landay
Designer:
Theo Louca
Director:
Carlos Soto
Creative Director:
Lorenzo De Rita
ID:
04043N

AGENCY Fuel Europe/Amsterdam
CLIENT Volvo Car Corporation

Talk a little about the creative process.

A number of concepts developed and exposed to consumers reinforced the provocative appeal of our creative approach and its potential to move consumers to re-evaluate their current opinions about Volvo and the new S40.

Our final solution was to promote a documentary film about "The Mystery of Dalarö," an investigation into the purported phenomenon of 32 people in a small Swedish village buying the S40 on the same day. The centerpiece of the mix was the online documentary and all channels drove consumers to view the documentary on Volvo's Web site. This revolutionary construct made a clear break from the conventions of premium automotive advertising and radically influenced the form and content of the message in each medium.

The (seemingly) unofficial documentary from Carlos Soto introduced a second, highly controversial campaign layer by fueling the central debate around "who's selling what in Dalarö and who's buying it?"

The interaction between all campaign elements, especially between the official and unofficial documentaries, provided many entry points into the campaign for consumers to explore the multiple layers of the "mystery" further. This was crucial aspect of winning the share of mind battle within the target group.

Talk a little about the documentary filming.

Although there was a detailed concept and script, it was crucial for the content and form to adhere to the production values of a real documentary. Therefore, Director Spike Jonze, Volvo and Fuel Europe needed to be able to respond to new ideas and capture them on film. One of the most crucial decisions was the interviews with real inhabitants from Dalarö. The improvised dialogue of them proved to be more effective than originally selected actors.

This is just one example of how a highly creative approach to the concept development was reflected to the same extent in every aspect of campaign production.

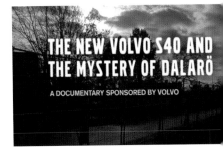

Art Directors:
Crystal English, Ray Andrade
Writers:
Quentin Shuldiner, Matt Rivitz,
Kevin Frank, Paul Venables
Photographers/Illustrators:
Geoff McFetridge, Ian Kovalik
Programmers:
Mike Heu, Koichiro Kamoji
Agency Producer:
Craig Allen
Production Company:
Mekanism
Producers:
Pete Caban, Stephanie Smith,
Tommy Means
Designer:
Ian Kovalik
Directors:
Geoff McFetridge, Ian Kovalik
Creative Directors:
Greg Bell, Paul Venables
ID:
04044N

**The new Napster launch was hotly anticipated.
Describe the client's brief and your execution of it.**
Our goal was to tease Napster's relaunch without overmarketing
and killing the brand's underground cachet. We wanted the old Napster
users to see our ads—whatever they would be—and instantly know we
were speaking to them in a way a mainstream advertiser never would.

So we decided to just tell the Napster story, but only funnier and
animated. The story would unfold episodically on a bare-bones Web site
(napsterbits.com) with banners teasing each new episode. We kept the site
relatively quiet. We wanted people to discover this work for themselves.
Or at the very most, be nudged in that direction.

As for execution, we tried to keep the episodes feeling raw and
underproduced. The flat simplicity of Flash immediately felt right for Napster,
as did Geoff McFetridge's simple yet smart as hell design style. And by adding
camera moves to the simple 2-D art, we got an engaging, cinematic look while
staying far away from the slick world of traditional animation.

The rest of the campaign, especially its offline components, came later,
closer to launch day. But anything that smelled of advertising, where all the
campaign pieces fit together too neatly, seemed wrong to us, like it was trying
too hard. So throughout the entire campaign—online animations, banners,
print, outdoor and TV—our only messaging was, "It's coming back." That's all
we really had to say.

What was the objective of the integrated branding campaign?

Alaska Airlines is a smaller airline that clings to the novel idea that customers still matter. To serve as a symbol of some of their not-so-considerate competitors, Alaska created the barely-parody SkyHigh Airlines, a shining example all that is wrong with the "friendly" skies.

To make SkyHigh even more painfully true-to-life, we created the (seemingly) fully functional skyhighairlines.com. Features include a Global Baggage Tracker, a monthly column written by SkyHigh's CEO, Howard Barium, and a working flight booking engine that invariably routes you through a handful of U.S. ghost towns. Visitors to the site could also sign up to receive emailed SkyHigh news and Howard Barium's "Mission Statement of the Week."

TV spots featured a businessman forced to try SkyHigh's new steerage-style "bench seating." Radio spots included the announcement of SkyHigh's exciting new "Random Gate-change Workout," whereby passengers would shed unwanted pounds simply by trying to catch their flight.

Every element of the integrated campaign was designed to show passengers that Alaska knows just how insanely frustrating air travel can be these days. And by doing so, we positioned Alaska as the airline that cares a bit more about making them happy.

Art Director:
Pam Fujimoto
Writers:
Matt McCain, John Schofield,
Jonathan Ozer
Photographer/Illustrator:
Pam Fujimoto
Programmers:
Steve Karr, Jeremy Fisher
Digital Artist/Multimedia:
Pam Fujimoto
Agency Producer:
Dax Estorninos
Production Company:
JGF
Producer:
Damian Stevens
Designer:
Pam Fujimoto
Information Architects:
Steve Karr, Jeremy Fisher
Director:
Jeff Gorman
Creative Director:
Tracy Wong
ID:
04045N

agency WONGDOODY/Seattle
client Alaska Airlines

CELEBRATION IS AS IMPORTANT AS THE GOAL ITSELF

Art Director:
Rasmus Frandsen
Writer:
Lewis Raven
Programmer:
Jesper Arvidson
Digital Artist/Multimedia:
Titoonic
Producer:
Caroline Bendixen
Designer:
Anders Gustafsson
Information Architect:
Jens Christiansen
Creative Director:
Lars Bastholm
URL:
http://nikefootball.nike.com/nikefootball/
front/celebration/index.jsp
ID:
04046N

The motion of the celebrating players is very natural. How did you capture it and what were some other technical challenges during production?

Soccer addicts know their celebrations and could spot fakes a mile off. So, it was essential that our animations matched-up to the moves pulled off by real players post-scoring. Unable to use and manipulate real footage of professional players celebrating, we had to reenact all the celebration moves we wanted. We got our raw footage using motion capture technology and two Capoeira dancers who used to play soccer semi-professionally. Having trussed up one of the guys with the necessary motion capture sensors and cables, we set about choreographing the moves.

What was the reaction from the users like? Discuss some of the feedback.

The huge number of matches played speaks for itself. A typical user comment was that the celebrations were cool and that they liked to score because the celebration part gave them the opportunity to really rub their opponent's nose in it.

agency Framfab/Copenhagen
client Nike Europe

**Talk about the client's brief and discuss your success
in translating the client's ideas.**

"Score with style, celebrate with style" was the campaign message. Building
on the related retail brochure, which focused on the most creative and
irreverent pro-player celebrations, Nike wanted us to take the concept further
by getting users to engage with these celebrations.

Our response was to develop a framework where users could create their
very own celebration online and then use it in a game against friends. Users
could select their styles from 24 different celebrations. Once complete,
users can proceed into a multiplayer game and take their celebration out into
the larger football community. When a user scores a goal, their celebration
plays out for both to see. With this, we feel we've brought the energy of the
celebration off the pitch and took it online.

A GAME OF TAG THROUGH A CITY OF TYPOGRAPHY

Through a series of simple behaviors, DoubleYou Barcelona was able to transport the user to a series of smartly designed streets where cursors hide, run, avoid and attack.

Art Director:
Blanca Piera
Writers:
Joakim Borgström, Esther Pino,
Daniel Solana
Programmers:
Jordi Martínez, Álvaro Sandoval,
Joakim Borgström
Digital Artist/Multimedia:
Mauricio Mazzariol
Producers:
Jordi Pont, Juan Pablo Pedemonte
Designer:
Elisabeth Badía
Creative Directors:
Joakim Borgström, Esther Pino,
Daniel Solana
URL:
http://www.doubleyou.com/festivals/
nikeplay/oneshow.html
ID:
04047N

Can you describe some of the technical challenges and successes of the piece?
The first challenge we faced was the creation of a stage where the cursors could move through it as well as a stage to block the way from the cursors to enter into the "buildings." As a solution, we used dot-matrix representation techniques and simple algebra calculations.

The next challenge was the implementation of the Artificial Intelligence of the cursors that live in the city and run away from the cursor. Bearing in mind we should create an experience that let us play, we decided to reject the more complex algorithms which overloaded the processor and slowed down the play; we chose to program simple behaviors that, put together, made the feeling of being in front of a crowd that hides, avoids, runs away and attacks you.

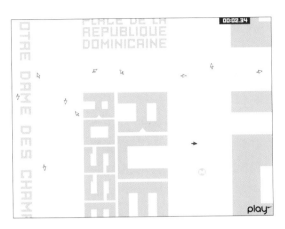

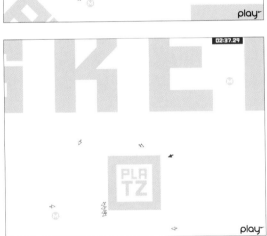

Another question was how to program the cursor intelligence that pursues you, once you have hunted it. Its ability to see you and increase its speed as time goes by increases the excitement of the pursuit.

Another technical issue we had to tackle was the integration of sound to create the same atmosphere as the original spot. We solved it by dissecting the original melody in different tracks that were put together smoothly, having as a reference the speed of the hunter cursor.

In the end, there were code lines we did not implement since we decided that it would slow down the game on most computers. The end result was programmed in a combination of maths, physics, and, above all, ingenuity.

A HIGH-SPEED CLASH OF THE TEEN TITANS

Using Shockwave, Pop & Co. was able to capture all of the colorful, high-speed action of Cartoon Network's popular Teen Titans series in this playable and fully loaded online game.

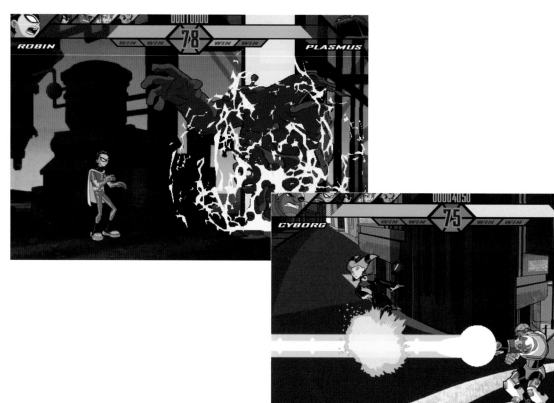

Art Director:
Jesse McGowan
Photographer/Illustrator:
Chuck Gammage
Programmer:
Michael Szabo
Producers:
Kelly Galligan, Demetri Detsaridis
Designer:
Scott Gursky
Creative Director:
Vincent Lacava
URL:
http://popandco.com/archive/titans
ID:
04048N

agency Pop & Co./New York
client Cartoon Network

PUMA AND POP PUT ONLINE GAMING ON THE GRID

In this stylish online game designed by Pop & Co., users can maneuver a runner armed with PUMA's USP technology through an expansive grid with environmental obstacles.

Art Director:
Jesse McGowan
Programmer:
Ted Warner
Producers:
Kelly Galligan, Demetri Detsaridis
Information Architect:
Frank Lantz
Creative Director:
Vincent Lacava
URL:
http://www.popandco.com/
archive/puma_usp
ID:
04049N

TOTAL GLOBAL DOMINATION AND THE ONLINE EXPERIENCE

Using irony to convey an important social issue to teens,
ScreenPlay created a gaming experience tied to a larger
Web campaign to educate kids about the dangers of smoking.

Smoking is an important youth issue.
Were you worried that making a game would be
misconstrued by some?
We had to worry about making our message as crisp as possible and, at the
same time, thrive to capture the audience so that they actually wanted to
listen to our message.

Irony is used throughout the game and in doing so, there will always be a
certain risk of misconception. But since the game is closely tied to other
campaign elements with a bona-fide approach, the danger of misconception is
strongly lessened.

Talk about technical execution.
During development we tried different angles of dramatizations of the
game, but found out that using real quotes and phrases from real tobacco
spokesmen using an ironic angle gave the strongest effect, which is stronger
than fiction.

Another important aspect was the game play. We decided to use a traditional
board game style that everyone can relate to, thus we were able to get the
audience into game play reasonably fast. The game is produced in Flash 6 and
communicated via several databases in order to put up score lists, etc. The
game also included a sophisticated advertising machine in which you could
generate your own tobacco ad(s) and send it to a friend via e-mail.

Art Directors:
Rune Glad, Daniel Senn
Programmer:
Andre Elvan
Producer:
Sveinung Totland
Designer:
Helge Tennø
Creative Director:
Rune Glad
URL:
http://www.screenplay.no/one/baron
ID:
04050N

**What audiences was the campaign directed towards
and how did they respond?**

The game was part of a large site covering all topics on the worldwide
tobacco industry. The site itself was part of a larger campaign covering print
and TV. The game's target audience was young people between the ages of 15
to 25, both smokers and non-smokers. The campaign lasted for four weeks.
There were over 130 thousand visitors to the game (which is quite many in
Norway!) with an average time spent of approximately five minutes, although
some actually played for hours. On launch day, a school class gave the game
two thumbs up during an interview on national television.

A PUBLIC ART AUCTION FOR THE WIRELESS WORLD

One of the first public auctions of its kind, London's Poke used SMS wireless technology to help Britart.com literally stop people in their tracks to appreciate the wonders of both art and technology.

Art Director:
Laurence Thompson
Writer:
Leon Wilson
Programmer:
Flytxt
Digital Artist/Multimedia:
Poke
Producer:
Nick Farnhill
Designer:
Laurence Thompson
Creative Directors:
Robert Saville, Matthew Clark
URL:
http://www.pokelondon.com/britart
ID:
04052N

Can you talk about some of the technical issues and technical objectives of holding an SMS auction?

The key technical issue regarding the operation of the auction was how to manage the issue of validating a bid from a cell phone. We wanted to validate bids as quickly as possible to allow people to get caught up in the enthusiasm of bidding for a piece of art. The original vision was to turn the cell phone into the bidding "paddle" with as few obstacles as possible presented to the bidder—the main objective being to mimic the auction room "energy" on a public pavement.

However, although a "request to bid" can be made via SMS, we needed to validate all "first-time" bidders to ensure that we weren't accepting bogus, or hoax, bids. The only way to validate each "first-time" bidder was via online at a later point in time. This wasn't ideal, but it did allow us to ensure that the bid was genuine by authorizing a credit card and registering the individual's details and cell phone number. So, although there was a break in the user experience when their "first bid" was made and processed—once each user had been validated they were able to bid directly from their cell phone and could then participate in any ensuing bidding wars.

**This was the world's first SMS auction via cell phone.
How did the public respond?**

Visually, the Very Public Art Gallery with the artists' work dominating every window of Selfridges was enormously impressive, literally stopping people in their tracks as they walked by. This in itself was a significant step towards presenting the Britart vision-of providing a source of affordable, well-known British art and offering a far more accessible means of enjoying these works.

This visual assault when partnered with the ubiquitous technology of SMS significantly improved people's perception of the consumption of art and generated an extremely positive response and critical comment. So, as a promotional piece championing Britart, British art, artists and Selfridges, this was a tremendous success.

In terms of sales, the work ranged in reserve price from £500 to over £12,000. As expected people were more inclined to participate in the lower value auctions and these proved to be most active. However, there were five items sold at a considerable premium—an unexpected but hugely welcome result.

How did the client respond to the work?

What was the client's brief?

Britart is dedicated to bringing the work of both emerging and established British artists to a wider audience. They believe that art should inspire the masses and that buying original art should not be an intimidating experience. To achieve this vision new, methods of access to and consumption of art must be devised.

Mother and Poke developed an intriguing new way to engage people through a simple technology (SMS) and one of the world's greatest retail stores (Selfridges). This combination proved to be very persuasive. Britart judged the project to be an enormous success in terms of underlining their innovative instincts, increasing their public profile and in creating fresh debate about the work of their artists. They also felt that a commercial objective had been achieved through the sale of a number of high value pieces.

britart.com

Home | **Browse art** | Search | Exhibitions | Magazine | My Britart | Mailing list

very public art gallery™   THE ART AUCTION WHERE YOU NOD WITH YOUR MOBILE

For those of you who cannot make it to a Selfridges store window we have all the works available in the auction right here. There will be a daily update of the current bidding prices posted here shortly after 5pm.

To make a bid, text BID, followed by the reference next to the work you want, along with the amount you want to bid for it in sterling, to the following phone number 83125. For example a bid of £2,000 for Josie McCoy's 'Pauline Fowler' would appear like this: BID MCC 2000.

To view the work at a larger size, for more details and more from this artist just click on your desired image.

   Code and current bid:
CAR £1,530

   Code and current bid:
DRO £1,100

   Code and current bid:
LIS £11,600
(Diptych see work
opposite)

   Code and current bid:
LIS £11,600
(Diptych see work
opposite)

   Code and current bid:
FIE £7,750

   Code and current bid:
MAR £1,900

britart.com two weeks home trial

Home | Browse art | New@Britart | Personal Services | Search | My Britart | Mailing list

start
here

artists
catalogue
& themed
galleries

   popup
buyers
guide

new@britart

search for art

join My Britart

offline gallery

britart@ eb**Y** .co.uk   Frank Worth Collection

107,985,78.5
Diesel Market Research
Clips installed

Browse artists by

britart.com

Home | Browse art | Search | Exhibitions | Magazine | My Britart | Mailing list

very public art gallery™   THE ART AUCTION WHERE YOU NOD WITH YOUR MOBILE

britart has teamed up with Selfridges to provide a very public art auction. The windows of the stores in both London and Manchester each feature one work available for you to bid for, by text message.

If you have already made your bid, we now need to confirm your phone number and credit/debit card details here. Once you have registered you can continue bidding on as many pieces as you like, as often as you want using that phone.

Click here to Validate Your Bid (this is a secure connection)

Click here to view the full Terms & Conditions

If you've yet to text your bid get to your nearest Selfridges store or click here to view the auction pieces.

Auction Closes
15 April 2003

SELFRIDGES&CO
London
Oxford Street
Manchester
Exchange Square
Trafford

A SCAVENGER HUNT FOR THE FOOTBALL CRAZY KIDS

Using SMS technology, AKQA created a wireless scavenger hunt in the streets of Sydney to turn young football fans on to the 2003 Rugby World Cup held in Australia.

Art Director:
Daniel Varon
Writer:
David Fullarton
Illustrator:
Darren Spiller
Programmer:
Gora Sundindranath
Digital Artists/Multimedia:
Daniel Varon, Joshua Sullivan,
Peter Cole, Mike Knott
Agency Producer:
Jamie Goodyear
Information Architect:
Sophie Henry
Creative Directors:
Glen Sheehan, Adam Lau
URL:
http://sf.akqa.com/awards/
oneshow04/
ID:
04053N

What was the objective of the campaign?
The Rugby World Cup is the 3rd largest sporting event in the world behind World Cup Soccer and the Summer Olympics. In October and November of 2003, the competition came to Australia. The marketing challenge was to get FCKs (Football Crazy Kids) excited about a sport that they had very little connection to, and all with no sports marketing access to the Australian rugby team. Our goal was to drive a deeper connection with our FCKs by giving them the opportunity to get actively involved with the sport. AKQA came up with a simple, yet fully integrated SMS game that kids could participate in solely through their mobile phones. No registration on the site was required to participate. Players embarked on a race to collect five icons placed around Sydney on posters, transit signs and stickers. The five icons represented five special skills or attitudes around rugby and each icon has its own SMS code. The goal of the Keep The Ball Alive campaign (KTBA) was to collect all five icons and collect prizes along the way.

agency AKQA/San Francisco
client Nike

Talk about the technical execution

In this rare, two-way mobile messaging campaign, players registered through SMS by sending the word "LIVE" to numbers listed on posters, signs and stickers. The return message included a voice recording from a rugby star as well as directions to a Web site where players could get instructions, track their progress, and receive rewards in the form of downloadable wallpapers and ring tones for mobile devices. While the game itself was played solely through SMS, all mobile content was delivered through third party content providers. Some of the challenges in this included working with multiple content providers and multiple carriers in the region, plus formatting this content for use on a range of handsets. Every 8-9 days, a new code was released on the streets. And if a player fell behind, they would automatically receive hints or directions to TV programs or Web sites where the missing code could be found.

PROVIDING PANTONES WITH PERSONALITY

The creative team at IAAH gave themselves the daunting directive to provide Pantone color chips with personality. As they fly across the screen and settle into place, you'll see that they succeeded.

Art Director:
Nessim Higson
Programmer:
Jared Lyvers
Digital Artist/Multimedia:
Matt Cross
Producers:
Bryant Fernandez, Nessim Higson
Designer:
Nessim Higson
Information Architects:
Jared Lyvers, Nessim Higson
Creative Director:
Bryant Fernandez
URL:
www.imustcreate.com
ID:
04054N

Describe the creative process and technical challenges faced by the team.

The Pantone chip came about when Art Director Ness and I were discussing the difficulties of holding our audience long enough to view the entire site. We decided we needed some kind of industry related mnemonic. Normally, you associate the chips as a color specifier, but we thought, what if the chip had a personality of sorts—one you could interact with? Hmm? (Please picture us rubbing our chins.)

Because of the realistic look of the animated chips created in Lightwave, a major concern was keeping it bandwidth friendly. It took many trials and errors and late nights before we finally got it right.

agency IAAH/New Orleans
client IAAH/FUTAGO

What are some of your favorite aspects of the site?

Immediately after the launch, we started receiving e-mails from all over the world. Mostly people wanted to know how the hell we made the chips fall into place like that—"Did you use strings?" "Did you shoot it up-side-down with a DV camera?" One guy had a bet with his roommate about it. He said they nearly came to blows over it. "Less filling!" "Tastes great!" Others just wanted to say, "nice work."

The most gratifying experience of the project was the collaboration that occurred between the four of us. Remove any one person and the project wouldn't be nearly as successful. Surely, one of the most rewarding and enjoyable projects any of us have worked on.

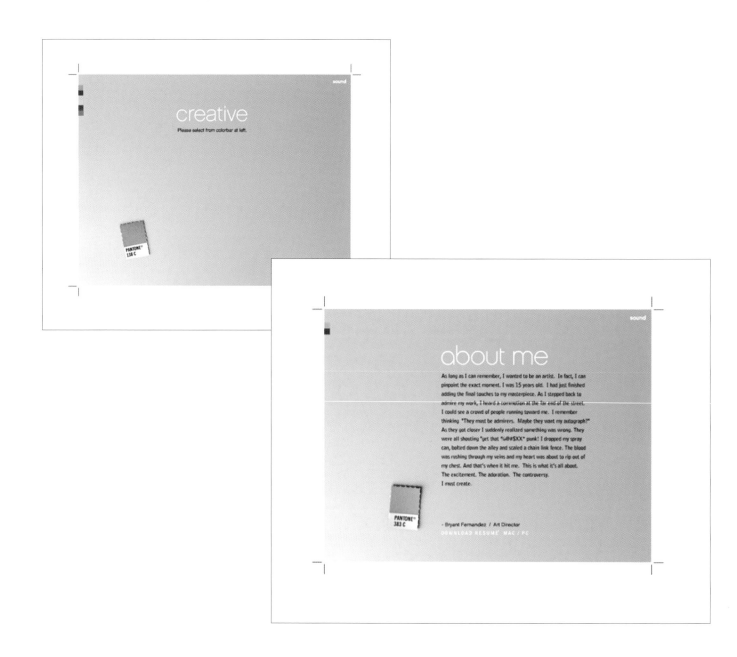

Interesting Facts.

From concept to completion the project took approximately three months to complete.

The software applications that were used to produce the site were Lightwave, Photoshop, Imageready, Illustrator, Soundedit, QuarkXpress and Flash. The primary animation sequences were developed in Lightwave and imported into Flash where we ran a series of optimization tests to see how we could reduce file size while maintaining optimum quality.

The cumulative file size for the site is 2.8 MB, not including the additional external content (QuickTime movies and print pieces that load as they are prompted). If a user doesn't want to see video, or higher resolution print, they won't ever have to load more than 2.8 MB. With the external content, the site is 15 MB.

Agency IAAH/New Orleans
client IAAH/FUTAGO

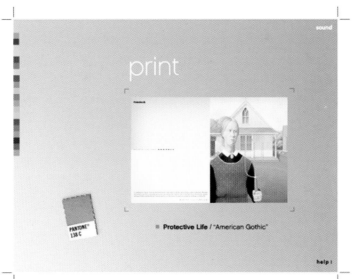

A WEB SITE GETS A QUICKTIME FACELIFT

Implementing QuickTime technology to enhance online usability, EyeballNYC created an eye-catching site with a browser-free interface that feels more like a media player than a typical Web site.

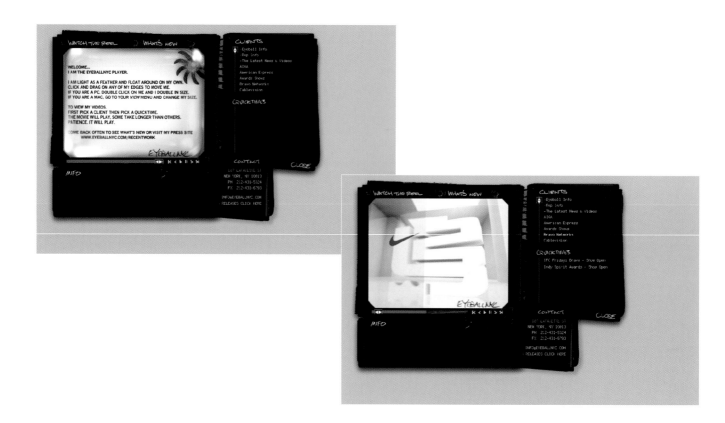

The Web site is one of the first to implement
QuickTime technology in such a unique application.
How did the creative team come up with this concept?
Our intention with our Web site is to show our work with the greatest of ease to our client. We prefer that there are no extra steps to get to our work. It should be immediately accessible. The QuickTime technology not only gave us that ease of use but it also gave us a unique and browser-free interface that felt more like a media player than a Web site. This player supported the individuality that is reflected in our work and our ideals.

What were some of the technical challenges involved
in working with such a new format for a Web site?
I think the most challenging aspect of our site was de-programming our users to accept this new and simpler approach to presenting our work.

How did users react to the work?
Our users never really reacted, either good or bad. This to us was the best response. It just worked and that was our goal.

Art Director:
Julian Bevan
Programmer:
Chuck Massucci
Digital Artist/Multimedia:
Last Exit
Production Company:
EyeballNYC
Producer:
Nuri Djavit
Designer:
Limore Shur
Information Architect:
Ken Negard
Creative Director:
Limore Shur
URL:
www.eyeballnyc.com
ID:
04055N

Agency EyeballNYC/New York
Client EyeballNYC

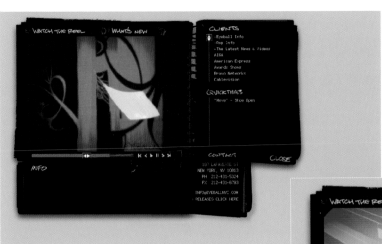

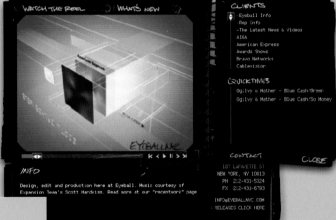

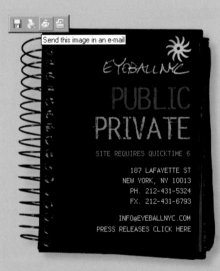

A DIRECTOR'S SHOW REEL SITE THAT'S THE CAT'S MEOW

UNIT 9 and Gorgeous collaborated to produce a whimsical method to add humor to the typical director's show reel using lovable kittens. Who doesn't love kittens?

Some sites make an immediate impression on the user by taking them on a highly innovative exploration of new technologies. Others display a keen sense of art direction, using fixed and animated graphic interfaces to leave users mesmerized and inspired. Other sites are rich in content and thus provide the user with information that can be accessed and applied to a host of different environments. Then there's a site the one produced by Unit 9 for Gorgeous, one of the premier production companies in the world responsible for some of the most memorable and moving television commercials of recent memory.

The simple, clean design and feline theme that runs throughout are not only charming and humorous, but more importantly presents the site in a usable manner that squarely puts the attention on the archived video clips of the six featured directors. A site made to showcase work of individual directors should be about the directors, not flashy Web animation or conceptual navigation. It is a tool for potential clients, but also a modes archive of commercial work for fans of advertising. The importance is usability, but that doesn't necessitate that the sight needs to follow in line with the cookie-cutter sites representing other production companies. And while UNIT 9 and Gorgeous took a chance on a whimsical site concept, they have landed squarely on their feet.

Art Director:
Frank Budgen
Writer:
Tom Carty
Programmers:
Steven Tilkin, Robert Bader, Tony Volpe
Producers:
Piero Frescobaldi, Mark Iremonger
Designer:
Katharina Leuzinger
Information Architect:
David Yates Buckley
Creative Director:
Chris Palmer
URL:
www.gorgeous.co.uk
ID:
04056N

USING ANIMATED MOVIES TO ENHANCE A WEB BRAND

Talk about the technical execution of the site. What were some of the challenges?

The production of this site was a long one because of the time required to design and animate the characters. Jim Hebb, our Senior Animator from The Embassy (theembassyvfx.com) worked for months creating the unique style the characters have. They move and bend in ways that seem to defy gravity, but at the same time they have a realistic quality to them. This was achieved through motion studies (watching fat people), acting the scripts out in the office, falling backwards on beds (one of them broke), and generally having a good time with it. The net result was the unique body language of our characters.

The site is presented in Flash 6, taking advantage of the ability to embed movie files within the larger presentation. These movies randomly load and play creating a unique experience for each user. While one movie is playing, another will be loading in the background. The Flash script was structured so that all of them will play once before repeating, and the same movie will never play twice in a row.

Art Directors:
Alex Beim, Dean Lee, Bruce Sinclair
Writers:
Jessica Raya, James Lee
Programmer:
Dana Brousseau
Digital Artist/Multimedia:
Jim Hebb
Producer:
Christi Rae
Designers:
Alex Beim, Dana Brousseau
Creative Directors:
Bruce Sinclair, Alan Russell
URL:
www.pjddb.com
ID:
04057N

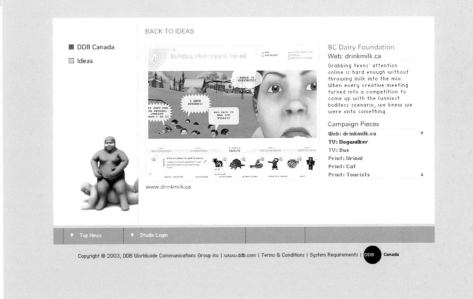

What was the objective of the Web site?

Our goal with the DDB Web site was to simplify how we present ourselves, and to showcase great work.

Describe the creative process and the responsibilities of each team member.

The art director and copywriter developed the site's overall concept and each scene. The animator was consulted on what was doable, and what would look the best. The Flash programmer was consulted on how to make the visuals more broadcast-like, with smooth and quick loading times. The producer beats some sense into the team as to what is doable and in what timeline.

A NEW VISION
OF THE ANNUAL
CORPORATE
X-MAS CARD

How was the piece distributed and to whom was it sent?
We had three main groups of people to send this message to: our clients, our suppliers and our friends. The brief that Martin and Simon got was media-neutral. We were simply looking for a new idea on the most dreaded project in the advertising industry—the annual company Christmas card. After a week or two they had exactly one concept. It seemed like a good one. There was never really any discussion about how we would deliver the goods. The only possible reason to put it on TV was so we could enter it in that particular catagory for the festivals (and that would be unthinkable, wouldn't it?) The original plan was to mail it directly as an mpeg, but because of firewalls and the large file size, we decided to send an e-mail invitation to view it on a Web site—with a link included.

We didn't believe this decision was a big deal, and that is a nice testimony to how far interactive communications have come. There were no feelings of euphoria about breaking new ground or reservations about using non-traditional media. We didn't even think twice about it.

Art Director:
Simon Staub
Writer:
Martin Stulz
Programmer:
Claude Schaub
Agency Producer:
Evelyn Doessegger
Production Company:
Chocolate Films
Producer:
Michela Trümpi
Director:
Benjamin Kempf
Creative Directors:
Keith Loell, Mark Stahel
ID:
04058N

Talk about the technical execution and the increased ease of using video in new media work.

Basically, the project could never have happened without doing it on video. Beni Kempf shot the whole thing with a digital camera over the course of a weekend. The talent is actually our handy-man, Maurice Barfuss. His range may be limited, but what he does, he does brilliantly. We treated it exactly like a film project after that. We did quite a bit of color work and edited it like any other TV commercial at Treib House, an online post-production studio. Same with the sound design—which was done by Philip and Moritz. When you look at it on a big screen you can certainly tell it's not film, but on the computer it's almost impossible to see the difference, which is kind of interesting. What's often percieved (rightly so) as a limitation of the media actually works to the advantage of lower-budget projects.

How did the users respond?

As far as we can tell, almost everyone who recieved the e-mail actually visited the site and saw the movie. We all got e-mails with compliments from people who weren't on the original mailing list. We found it on a couple of industry blogs. And most importantly, none of us got any annoying calls from the clients over the holiday break.

agency Lowe AG/Zurich
client Lowe AG

THE PROGRESSION OF TIME IN A LINEAR MODEL

As a New Year's present to friends and customers, Germany's Scholz & Volkmer created a linear clock in Flash 6 that shows the fleeting nature of time.

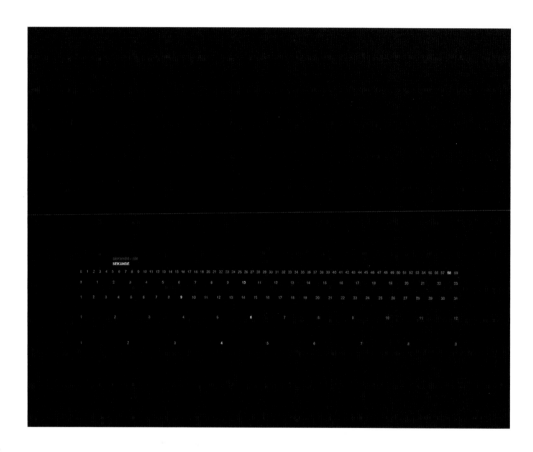

Discuss some of the technical issues of the execution. What software was used in the production?
The Timesaver was originally written in C++ some years ago and now has been ported to Flash 6.

Talk about the objectives of the piece.
The Timesaver presents the progression of time in a linear instead of a cyclic fashion and therefore shows the fluidity of time and each of its moments.

Who was sent the Timesaver and how did the users respond?
Timesaver was sent to customers and friends of Scholz & Volkmer as a New Year's present. They loved it.

Art Director:
Anne Wichmann
Programmers:
Manfred Kraft, Peter Reichard
Production Company:
Scholz & Volkmer
Information Architects:
Manfred Kraft, Peter Reichard,
Michael Volkmer
Creative Director:
Michael Volkmer
URL:
www.s-v.de/timesaver
ID:
04059N

SOME HOLIDAY CHEER FOR THE DOG DAYS OF WINTER

Buddy
Aurora, Illinois

What was the objective of the piece?
In that it didn't have our phone number or address or any sort of call to action (except Buddy's plea for respectability), the primary objective of this short video we emailed was to wish our clients and friends a happy holiday season. But we also sent it to several potential clients just to pull Truth and Advertising a little closer towards the front of their minds and give our subsequent promotional pieces a little more stopping power.

Talk about technical challenges and triumphs.
What is the implementation of the piece?
Right at the time we put this together, we were also doing a television spot for which we were having an actor named Steve Morris do the voiceover (famous in our part of the world for some really funny local ski resort commercials). When we were finished recording the real spot, we asked if he wouldn't mind being the voice of our agency's holiday video email. He very kindly obliged, and his talents proved instrumental in the spot's appeal. I don't think we would've booked studio time and voice talent just for our agency holiday video, so what might have been our biggest challenge became a triumph by virtue of auspicious timing.

Art Director:
Shawn Gill
Writer:
Jason Allan
Programmer:
Joe Schwab
Digital Artist/Multimedia:
Joe Schwab
Designer:
Shawn Gill
Information Architect:
Joe Schwab
Creative Directors:
Joe Duffy, Doug Reeves, Tony Bever
URL:
http://www.truthandadvertising.com/
happyholidays/
ID:
04060N

agency Truth and Advertising/Santa Ana
client Truth and Advertising

Merit Winners

Banner — Single

Agency
AgênciaClick/São Paulo
Client
Coca-Cola Brasil

Art Director:
Fred Siqueira
Programmer:
Flavio Banyai
Producer:
Alessandra Baptista
Designers:
Fred Siqueira, Veni Cury
Creative Director:
PJ Pereira
URL:
http://awards.agenciaclick.com.br/
recyclingprogram/en
ID:
04067N

Banner — Single

Agency
AgênciaClick/São Paulo
Client
Coca-Cola Brasil

Art Directors:
Rodrigo Buim, Emerson Viegas
Writer:
Suzana Apelbaum
Producer:
Alessandra Baptista
Designers:
Emerson Viegas, Diego Zambrano
Creative Director:
PJ Pereira
URL:
http://awards.agenciaclick.com.br/
footbag/en
ID:
04068N

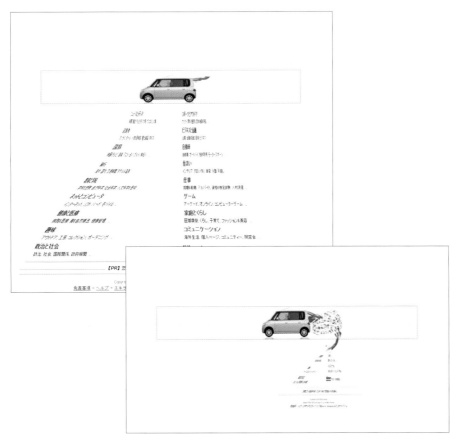

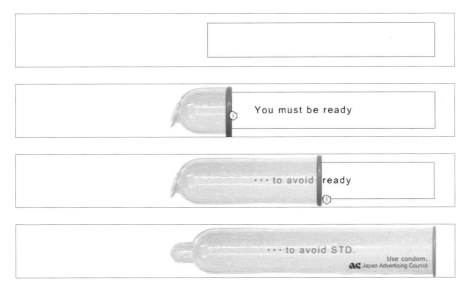

Banner — Single

agency
Dentsu/Tokyo
client
Diahatsu Motor

Art Director:
Yusuke Kitani
Writer:
Akihito Abe
Programmer:
Hiroki Nakamura
Producer:
Tomoko Yokota
Designer:
Yusuke Kitani
Director:
Hiroki Nakamura
Creative Director:
Akihito Abe
URL:
http://www.interactive-salaryman.com/
2004pieces/d0329E/index.html
ID:
04069N

You must be ready

··· to avoid ready

··· to avoid STD.
Use condom.
Japan Advertising Council

Banner — Single

agency
Dentsu/Tokyo
client
Japan Advertising Council

Art Directors:
Yusuke Kitani, Aco Suzuki
Writer:
Shoichi Tamura
Photographer/Illustrator:
Shinji Ashibe
Programmer:
Toshiyuki Onishi
Digital Artist/Multimedia:
Aco Suzuki
Producer:
Kazutaka Fukushima
Designers:
Shinji Ashibe, Yusuke Kitani
Creative Director:
Takeshi Mizukawa
URL:
http://www.interactive-salaryman.com/
2004pieces/d0303E/
ID:
04070N

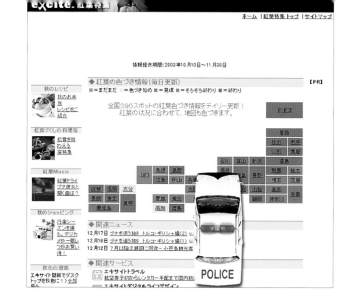

Banner — Single

Agency
Dentsu/Tokyo
Client
Japan Advertising Council

Art Director:
Kaori Mochizuki
Writer:
Akihito Abe
Programmer:
Hiroki Nakamura
Producer:
Tomoko Yokota
Designer:
Kaori Mochizuki
Director:
Hiroki Nakamura
Creative Director:
Akihito Abe
URL:
http://www.interactive-salaryman.com/
2004pieces/d0325E/
ID:
04071N

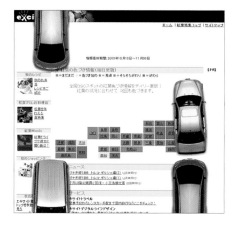 

Banner — Single

Agency
e-Crusade Marketing/
Quarry Bay
Client
Janssen Pharmaceutica

Designer:
Man Kit Au Yeung
Creative Director:
Endy Fung
URL:
http://www.e-crusade.com/
oneshow2004.jsp
ID:
04072N

Banner — Single

agency
Loducca Publicidade/
São Paulo
client
PURINA

Art Director:
Daniella Frojuello
Writer:
Paulo Fontana
Photographer/Illustrator:
Fabio Camargo
Producer:
Fabio Camargo
Designers:
Renato Frigo, Ricardo Schreier
Creative Directors:
Celso Loducca, Amaury Bali Terçarolli
URL:
http://www.lo-v.com/award/
oneshow2004/tail
ID:
04073N

Banner — Single

agency
Loducca Publicidade/
São Paulo
client
SCHERING

Art Director:
Amaury Bali Terçarolli
Writer:
André Piva
Programmer:
Marcio Quartilho
Producer:
Gisele Pereira
Designer:
Amaury Bali Terçarolli
Creative Directors:
Celso Loducca, Amaury Bali Terçarolli,
Anrdé Piva
URL:
http://www.lo-v.com/award/
oneshow2004/secure/
ID:
04074N

Banner — Single

agency
Neue Digitale/
Frankfurt am Main
client
JK's Tattoo & Piercing

Art Director:
Roanne Yee
Programmers:
Jens Steffen, Peter Kirsch
Creative Director:
Olaf Czeschner
URL:
http://www.neue-digitale.de/
awards/tattoo.html
ID:
04075N

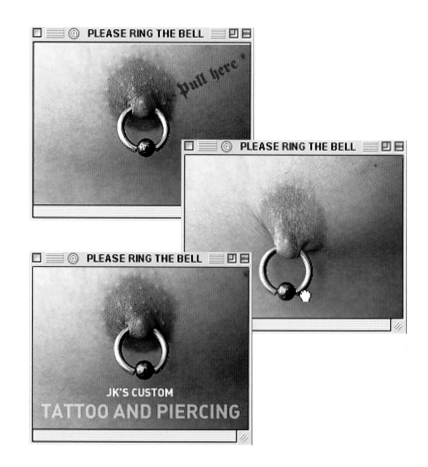

Banner — Single

agency
OgilvyInteractive worldwide/
São Paulo
client
IBM

Art Director:
Milton Correa Jr.
Writer:
Moacyr Guimarães Netto
Programmer:
Vincent Maraschin
Designers:
Milton Correa Jr., Cristiano Fernandes
Creative Directors:
Adriana Cury, Paulo Sanna
URL:
http://www.ogilvy.com.br/
ourwork2004/eyes
ID:
04115N

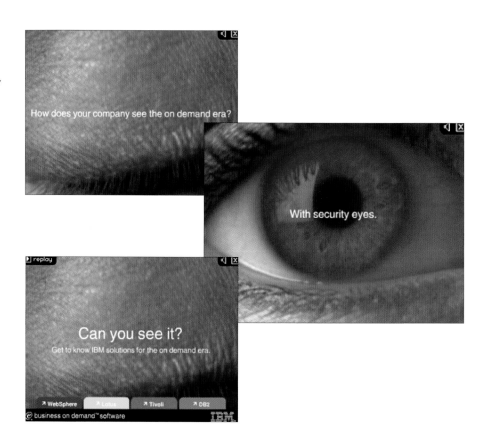

Banner — Single

Agency
OgilvyOne worldwide/
London
Client
IBM

Art Directors:
Howard Dean, Zak Loney
Writer:
David Shearer
Programmers:
Fraser Campbell, Gary Jobe,
Thorkild Clausen, Peter Lewis-Dale,
Harsha Yogasundrum
Producer:
Rebecca Mackenzie
Designers:
Zak Loney, Howard Dean
Creative Director:
Colin Nimick
URL:
http://www.creative-awards.co.uk/
oneshow03/ibmwimbledon/
ID:
04076N

Banner — Single

Agency
OgilvyOne worldwide/
Singapore
Client
GlaxoSmithKline

Art Directors:
Ashidiq Ghazali, Dominic Goldman
Writer:
Audra Tan
Programmer:
Chandra Barathi
Producer:
Yow Pin Fern
Designers:
Ashidiq Ghazali, Victor Ong
Creative Director:
Graham Kelly
URL:
http://www.our-work.com/
scotts/tall_boy.html
ID:
04077N

Banner — Single

Agency
OgilvyOne worldwide/
Singapore
client
Levi Strauss

Art Directors:
Ashidiq Ghazali, Dominic Goldman
Writer:
Audra Tan
Programmer:
Chandra Barathi
Producer:
Yow Pin Fern
Designers:
Dominic Goldman, Ashidiq Ghazali,
Shawn Loo
Creative Director:
Dominic Goldman
URL:
http://www.our-work.com/
levis/levis_wm.htm
ID:
04078N

Banner — Single

Agency
OgilvyOne worldwide/
Singapore
client
Nokia

Art Director:
Ashidiq Ghazali
Writer:
Audra Tan
Programmers:
Chandra Barathi, Colin Foo, Raju TV
Producer:
Memi Chang
Designer:
Arnold Widjanarko
Creative Director:
Dominic Goldman
URL:
http://www.our-work.com/nokia/
3200/banner/drag.htm
ID:
04079N

Click her face to discover
the difference Dove makes

Banner — Single

agency
OgilvyOne worldwide/
Singapore
client
Unilever

Art Directors:
Ashidiq Ghazali, Dominic Goldman
Writer:
Audra Tan
Programmer:
Chandra Barathi
Designers:
Steve Lawler, Victor Ong
Creative Director:
Graham Kelly
URL:
http://www.our-work.com/
dove/smooth
ID:
04080N

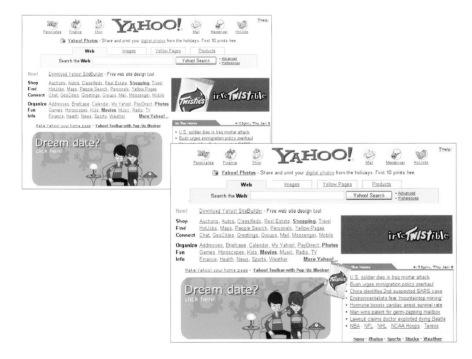

Banner — Single

agency
Saatchi & Saatchi/
Petaling Jaya
client
Danone Marketing

Art Directors:
Ong Kien Hoe, Henry Yap
Writers:
Ronald Ng, Raymond Ng
Programmer:
CUE Art & Design Associates
Designer:
CUE Art & Design Associates
Creative Director:
Edmund Choe
URL:
http://www.geocities.com/
twistiesbanner/
ID:
04081N

Banner — Single

Agency
Saatchi & Saatchi/
Wellington
client
Telecom NZ

Art Directors:
Tom Eslinger, Erik Hay
Writer:
Matthew Grainger
Programmer:
David Colquhoun
Producers:
Tracy Adams, Lara Bowen
Designers:
Erik Hay, Tom Eslinger
Creative Director:
Tom Eslinger
URL:
http://www.saatchinzonline.com/
passtheparcel
ID:
04083N

Banner — Single

Agency
Saatchi & Saatchi AtPlay/
Cape Town
client
Amnesty International

Art Directors:
Gavin Cromhout, Uwe Gutschow,
Mark Mason
Writers:
Conn Bertish, Uwe Gutschow,
Gavin Cromhout
Programmer:
Gavin Cromhout
Agency Producer:
Uwe Gutschow
Production Company:
Lodestone
Producer:
Uwe Gutschow
Designer:
Gavin Cromhout
Creative Directors:
Gavin Cromhout, Uwe Gutschow
URL:
http://www.saatchiatplay.com/
awards/expression/
ID:
04082N

Everyone ha

Everyone has the right to dom of expr

Everyone has the right to freedom of expression with

amnesty international
WORKING TO PROTECT HUMAN RIGHTS WORLDWIDE

Banner — Single

agency
TBWA\Chiat\Day\
TEQUILA/New York
client
Absolut

Art Director:
Doug Jaeger
Programmer:
Ze Frank
Agency Producer:
Richard Coughlin
Creative Director:
Doug Jaeger
URL:
http://interact.tbwachiat.com/
awards/oc04_jam/
ID:
04084N

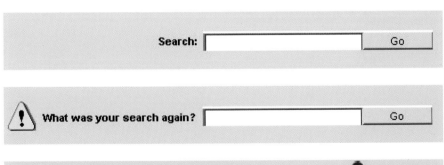

Banner — Single

agency
TBWA\Germany/Berlin
client
Alzheimer Research

Art Directors:
Rainer Schmidt, Donald Tursman
Writers:
Rainer Schmidt, Donald Tursman
Production Company:
TEQUILA\Germany
Director:
René Kriegler
Creative Director:
Kai Röffen
URL:
http://clio.tbwa.de/2004/
ID:
04085N

Banner — Single

AGENCY
Tribal DDB/Vancouver
CLIENT
BMO Investorline

Art Director:
Alex Beim
Writer:
Tony Nichols
Photographer/Illustrator:
Adam Rogers
Programmer:
Dana Brousseau
Digital Artist/Multimedia:
Kevin Long
Producers:
Christi Rae, Kimberly Clifford
Designer:
Dana Brousseau
Creative Director:
Bruce Sinclair
URL:
xn.tribalddb.ca
ID:
04086N

Banner — Single

AGENCY
Venables, Bell & Partners/
San Francisco
CLIENT
Napster

Art Director:
Crystal English
Writer:
Quentin Shuldiner
Illustrators:
Geoff McFetridge, Sam Hood
Agency Producer:
Craig Allen
Production Company:
Mekanism
Producers:
Pete Caban, Stephanie Smith
Designer:
Sam Hood
Director:
Ian Kovalik
Creative Directors:
Greg Bell, Paul Venables
URL:
http://www.napster.com/bits
ID:
04087N

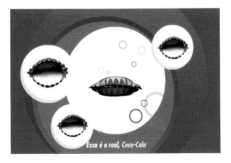

Banner — Single

agency
Venables, Bell & Partners/
San Francisco
client
Napster

Art Director:
Crystal English
Writer:
Quentin Shuldiner
Illustrator:
Ian Kovalik
Agency Producer:
Craig Allen
Production Company:
Mekanism
Producers:
Pete Caban, Stephanie Smith
Designers:
Ian Kovalik, Sam Hood
Director:
Ian Kovalik
Creative Directors:
Greg Bell, Paul Venables
URL:
http://www.napster.com/bits
ID:
04121N

Banner — Campaign

agency
AgênciaClick/São Paulo
client
Coca-Cola Brasil

Art Director:
Fred Siqueira
Writers:
PJ Pereira, Suzana Apelbaum
Programmer:
Flavio Banyai
Producer:
Alessandra Baptista
Designer:
Fred Siqueira
Creative Director:
PJ Pereira
URL:
http://awards.agenciaclick.com.br/
taps/en
ID:
04088N

Banner — Campaign

Agency
Berger Baader Hermes/
digital/Munich
client
HypoVereinsbank

Art Director:
Markus Beige
Writer:
Jörg Carsten Müller
Programmer:
Jörg Müller
Digital Artist/Multimedia:
Jörg Janda
Designers:
Markus Beige, Sabrina Hezinger,
Tobias Mayer
Creative Director:
Matthias Berger
URL:
http://www.bbh-digital.de/
awards/ny/oneshow.html
ID:
04089N

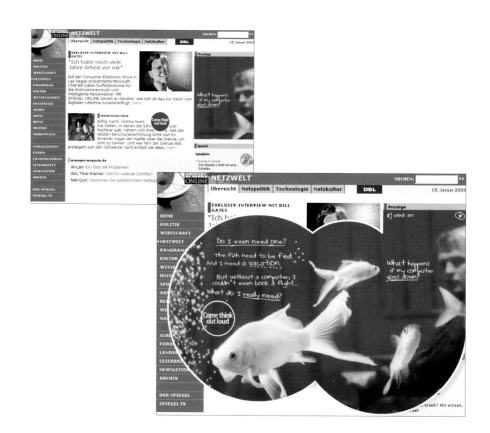

Banner — Campaign

Agency
Digitas/Boston
client
American Express

Art Director:
Jason Anello
Writer:
Doug Bost
Producer:
Ross Field
Creative Director:
Matt D'Ercole
URL:
http://newyork.digitas.com/blue
ID:
04090N

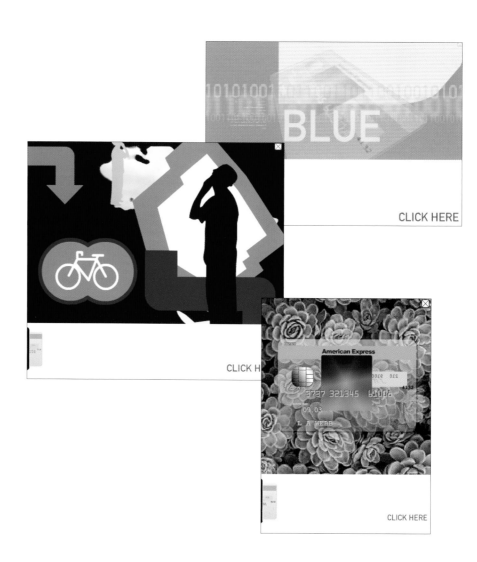

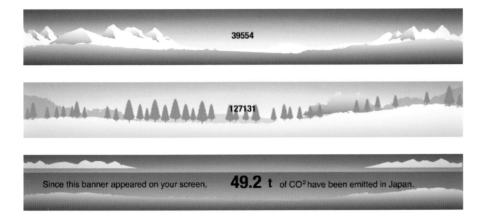

Banner — Campaign

AGENCY
Hakuhodo/Tokyo
client
World Wide Fund for
Nature Japan

Art Directors:
Takayoshi Kishimoto, Yuji Suzuki
Writers:
Toshiya Fukuda, Hiroko Ishii,
Michael Glenn
Photographer/Illustrator:
Yuji Suzuki
Programmer:
Tomoyuki Tada
Agency Producer:
Shinji Fukao
Production Company:
TYO Interactive Design
Producers:
Kenji Morimoto, Yutaka Sugiyama
Designer:
Yuji Suzuki
Information Architect:
Yukio Sato
Creative Director:
Toshiya Fukuda
URL:
http://www.tyo-id.co.jp/works/
banner/2003/wwf/05.html
ID:
04091N

Banner — Campaign

AGENCY
iLeo/Chicago
client
U.S. Army

Art Directors:
Zac Rybacki, Mike McCarthy,
Meghan DeRoma
Writer:
Todd Beeby
Digital Artist/Multimedia:
Mark Zelis
Producer:
Meghan McEwen
Creative Director:
Jamie Anderson
URL:
http://www.ileo.com/oneshow/
goarmy/2400_7
ID:
04092N

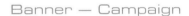

Banner — Campaign

agency
itraffic an AGENCY.COM
company/New York
client
Discovery Channel

Programmer:
J. L. Novosad
Designer:
Greg Smith
Director:
Damon Burrell
Creative Director:
Blair Shapiro
URL:
http://showcase.itraffic.com/
dinosaurplanet/campaign.html
ID:
04093N

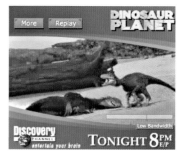

Banner — Campaign

agency
MRM Partners/
San Francisco
client
Microsoft

Art Director:
Kevin McMonagle
Writer:
Jenn Maer
Photographers/Illustrators:
Greg Roberts, Mike Cole
Programmer:
EVB
Digital Artists/Multimedia:
Greg Roberts, Mike Cole
Agency Producer:
Bill Prince
Production Company:
EVB
Producer:
Justin Acuff
Designers:
Greg Roberts, Mike Cole
Director:
Jason Zada
Creative Directors:
Mark Edwards, Burr Purnell
URL:
http://client.mrmgould.com/
oneshow/Office11W/
ID:
04094N

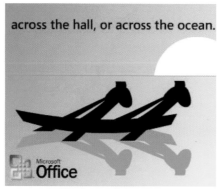

OKAY. NO MORE OF THESE.
PLEASE REFRAIN FROM BLACKMAILING
US FOR BOARDS.
IT JUST WONT HAPPEN.
WAIT FOR LAUNCH AND YOU CAN
WIN ONE. MAYBE.
PS. WE MEAN IT!

Banner — Campaign

AGENCY
Neue Digitale/
Frankfurt am Main
client
NITRO Snowboards

Art Director:
Rolf Borcherding
Writer:
Roland Grossmann
Creative Director:
Olaf Czeschner
URL:
http://www.neue-digitale.de/awards/
nitro-blackmail.html
ID:
04095N

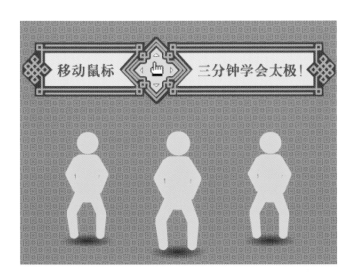

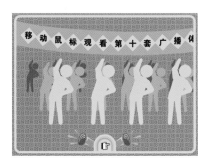

Banner — Campaign

AGENCY
OgilvyOne worldwide/
Beijing
client
China Mobile

Art Director:
Yang Yanyan
Writer:
Ivy Zhong
Programmer:
Fu Huaiying
Digital Artist/Multimedia:
Ryan Liu
Producer:
Liu Yifeng
Designer:
Eric Zhong
Information Architects:
Zhen Hao, Jin Yinghui
Creative Director:
Dirk Eschenbacher
URL:
http://210.73.87.152/work/
cmcc/launch/
ID:
04096N

Banner — Campaign

Agency
OgilvyOne worldwide/
Singapore
client
Nokia

Art Director:
Ashidiq Ghazali
Writer:
Audra Tan
Programmers:
Chandra Barathi, Colin Foo, Raju TV
Producer:
Memi Chang
Designer:
Arnold Widjanarko
Creative Director:
Dominic Goldman
URL:
http://www.our-work.com/nokia/
3200/banner/
ID:
04097N

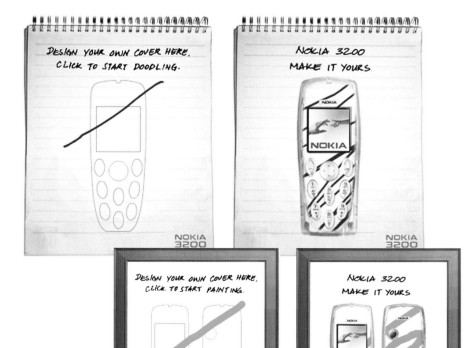

Banner — Campaign

Agency
Organic/Bloomfield Hills
client
Napster

Art Director:
Crystal English
Writers:
Ben Citron, Quentin Shuldiner
Producers:
Celia von Bernuth, John Kiladis
Designer:
Kelley Barry
Creative Director:
Christian Haas
URL:
http://awards.organic.com/napster
ID:
04098N

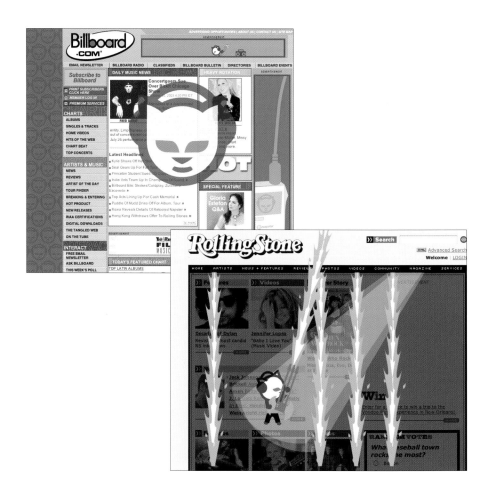

Banner — Campaign

Agency
Syrup/Chippendale
Client
Blackmores Limited

Art Director:
Ashadi Hopper
Writers:
Charlie Lawrence, Paul Fishlock
URL:
http://www.syrup.com.au/oneshow/
ID:
04099N

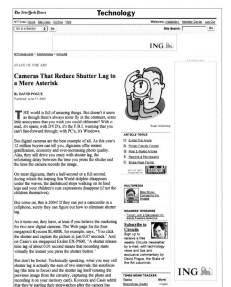

Banner — Campaign

Agency
Tribal DDB/
New York
Client
Tribal DDB/
New York

Art Director:
Daniel Modell
Writer:
Mark Bellusci
Programmer:
Danny Hobart
Creative Directors:
Duncan Mitchell, Brook Lundy
URL:
http://www.tribalddbny.com/
awards/break.html
ID:
04100N

Banner — Campaign

agency
Zentropy Partners/London
client
Tourism Ireland

Art Director:
Stuart Mcluskie
Writer:
Matt Hallet
Programmer:
Stephen Hamilton
Producer:
Lir Cowman
Creative Director:
Matt Mayes
URL:
http://www.zentropypartners.co.uk/
awards/2004/tourismireland/
ID:
04101N

Discover Ireland from your desk

The new Tourism Ireland website

Experience Ireland at the click of a button

Visit the new Tourism Ireland site

CLICK HERE

CLICK HERE

Ireland

Ireland

Ireland

Ireland

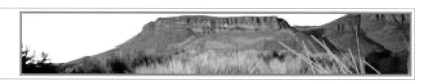

CLICK HERE

tourism**Ireland**.com

Beyond the Banner — Single

agency
AKQA/San Francisco
client
Nike

Art Director:
Daniel Varon
Writer:
Adam Lau
Illustrator:
Rostarr
Programmer:
Gora Sundindranath
Digital Artists/Multimedia:
Mike Knott, Peter Cole, Joshua Sullivan
Agency Producers:
Charlie Taylor, Peter Lenn
Designer:
Matthew Schneider
Information Architect:
Sophie Henry
Creative Directors:
Glen Sheehan, Adam Lau
URL:
http://sf.akqa.com/awards/oneshow04/
ID:
04102N

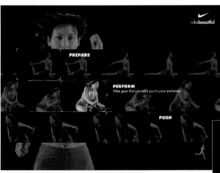

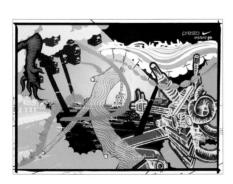

Beyond the Banner
— Single

agency
AKQA/San Francisco
client
Nike

Art Directors:
Bob Pullum, Satoko Furuta
Writers:
Shira Friedman, Janet Champ
Photographers:
Faubel Christensen, Guzman
Programmers:
Peter Cole, Gora Sundindranath
Digital Artists/Multimedia:
Daniel Varon, Joshua Sullivan, Peter Cole,
Mike Knott
Agency Producers:
Charlie Taylor, Peter Lenn
Designers:
Alysha Naples, Satoko Furuta, Chris Shipman
Information Architect:
Sophie Henry
Creative Directors:
Glen Sheehan, Bob Pullum
URL:
http://sf.akqa.com/awards/oneshow04/
ID:
04103N

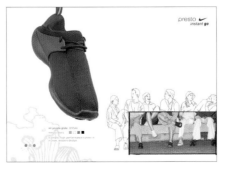

Beyond the Banner
— Single

agency
AKQA/San Francisco
client
Nike

Art Director:
Bob Pullum
Writer:
Adam Lau
Photographers/Illustrators:
David Ellis, Barnstormers
Programmer:
Gora Sundindranath
Digital Artists/Multimedia:
Mike Knott, Peter Cole, Joshua Sullivan
Agency Producers:
Charlie Taylor, Peter Lenn
Designer:
Alysha Naples
Information Architect:
Sophie Henry
Creative Director:
Glen Sheehan
URL:
http://sf.akqa.com/awards/oneshow04/
ID:
04104N

Beyond the Banner
— Single

Agency
AKQA/San Francisco
client
Nike

Art Directors:
Daniel Varon, Eddy Tolfsie,
Matthew Schneider, Matt Kipp
Writers:
Steve Scowden, Adam Lau
Programmers:
Peter Cole, Gora Sundindranath
Digital Artists/Multimedia:
Daniel Varon, Eddy Tolfsie, Matt Kipp,
Joshua Sullivan, Peter Cole, Mike Knott
Agency Producers:
Charlie Taylor, Peter Lenn
Creative Director:
Glen Sheehan
URL:
http://sf.akqa.com/awards/
oneshow04/
ID:
04105N

Beyond the Banner
— Single

Agency
AlmapBBDO/São Paulo
client
Audi

Art Directors:
Luiz Sanches, Fabio Costa
Writer:
Roberto Pereira
Programmer:
Paulo Pacheco
Creative Directors:
Marcello Serpa, Fabio Costa
URL:
http://www.almapbbdo.com.br/
awards/2004/audi/cabriolet/
ID:
04106N

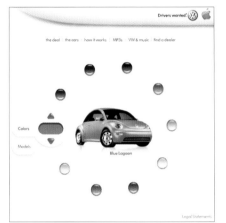

Beyond the Banner
— Single

Agency
Arnold Worldwide/Boston
Client
Volkswagen

Art Director:
Nicole McDonald
Writer:
Kerry Lynch
Programmer:
The Barbarian Group
Production Company:
The Barbarian Group
Producer:
Jen Bruns
Designer:
Cindy Moon
Information Architect:
Patrick Eddy
Creative Directors:
Ron Lawner, Alan Pafenbach, Tim Brunelle,
Chris Bradley, Dave Weist
URL:
http://awards.arn.com/iPod/index.html
ID:
04107N

Beyond the Banner
— Single

Agency
Arnold Worldwide/Boston
Client
Volkswagen

Art Director:
Nicole McDonald
Writer:
Rob Thompson
Programmer:
The Barbarian Group
Production Company:
The Barbarian Group
Producer:
Jen Bruns
Information Architect:
Patrick Eddy
Creative Directors:
Ron Lawner, Alan Pafenbach,
Chris Bradley, Tim Brunelle
URL:
http://www.vw.com/newModels.htm
(Click on New Beetle Convertible)
ID:
04131N

Beyond the Banner
— Single

Agency
Arnold Worldwide/Boston
client
Volkswagen

Art Directors:
Mike Gatti, Dmitri Cavander
Writer:
Kerry Lynch
Programmer:
The Barbarian Group
Producer:
Jen Iwanicki
Designer:
Will McGinness
Creative Directors:
Ron Lawner, Alan Pafenbach,
Tim Brunelle, Chris Bradley
URL:
http://www.vw.com/newModels.htm
(Click on Touareg)
ID:
04132N

Beyond the Banner
— Single

Agency
Bartle Bogle Hegarty/
New York
client
Unilever/Axe

Art Directors:
Jeff Church, Gianfranco Arena
Writers:
Brian Friedrich, Peter Kain
Agency Producer:
Josette Lata
Designer:
Matt Campbell
Creative Director:
William Gelner
URL:
http://www.theaxeeffect.com/
handbook/flash.html
ID:
04108N

Beyond the Banner — Single

agency
Fusebox/New York
client
ESPN The Magazine

Art Director:
Alan Buchanan
Writer:
Andy Carrigan
Programmer:
Alex Britez
Digital Artist/Multimedia:
Alex Britez
Designer:
Steve Newman
Creative Directors:
Steve Newman, Paul Renner,
Kevin Proudfoot
URL:
http://www.fusebox.com/fbx/client_
extranet/call_oneclub_2004.html
ID:
04109N

Beyond the Banner — Single

agency
Goodby, Silverstein &
Partners/San Francisco
client
Anheuser-Busch

Art Directors:
Todd Grant, Kris Wixom
Writers:
Steve Dildarian, Alisa Sengel
Photographers/Illustrators:
Steve Dildarian, Kris Wixom
Agency Producer:
James Horner
Information Architect:
Ted DePalma
Creative Directors:
Jeffrey Goodby, Rich Silverstein
URL:
http://www.goodbysilverstein.com/
one_show/spots.html
ID:
04110N

Beyond the Banner
— Single

Agency
Goodby, Silverstein &
Partners/San Francisco
Client
Anheuser-Busch

Art Directors:
Todd Grant, Kris Wixom
Writers:
Steve Dildarian, Alisa Sengel
Photographers/Illustrators:
Steve Dildarian, Kris Wixom
Agency Producer:
James Horner
Information Architect:
Ted DePalma
Creative Directors:
Jeffrey Goodby, Rich Silverstein
URL:
http://www.goodbysilverstein.com/
one_show/spots.html
ID:
04111N

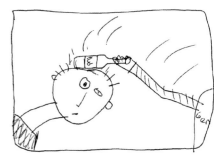

Beyond the Banner
— Single

Agency
Herraiz Soto & Co./
Barcelona
Client
BMW

Art Directors:
Angel Herraiz, Sergi Mula
Writer:
Rafa Soto
Photographer/Illustrator:
Jordi Duró
Programmers:
Carles Sanz, Javier Alvarez
Creative Directors:
Angel Herraiz, Rafa Soto
URL:
http://www.herraizsoto.com/
festivales/Z4web
ID:
04112N

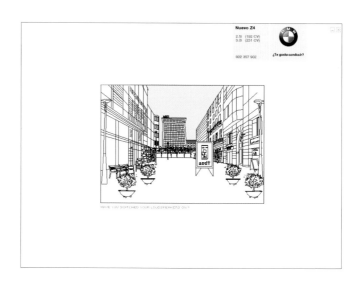
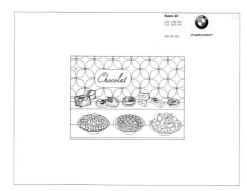

Beyond the Banner
— Single

Agency
J. Walter Thompson/Detroit
Client
Ford Motor Company

Art Directors:
Nicholas D'Angelo, Ken Tadeo
Writer:
Randy Campbell
Digital Artists/Multimedia:
Justin Mysza, Shane Mielke
Agency Producer:
Kim Blommer
Producer:
Samantha Burton
Designer:
Kevin McElroy
Information Architect:
Patrick Callow
Creative Directors:
Tom Cordner, Dave Garant,
Ken Tadeo
URL:
http://www.fordvehicles.com/
trucks/f-150
ID:
04142N

Beyond the Banner
— Single

Agency
Loducca Publicidade/
São Paulo
Client
2001 Videolocadora

Art Director:
Amaury Bali Terçarolli
Writer:
André Piva
Programmer:
Marcio Quartilho
Producer:
Gisele Pereira
Designer:
Amaury Bali Terçarolli, Jefferson Rocha
Creative Directors:
Celso Loducca, Amaury Bali Terçarolli,
André Piva
URL:
http://www.lo-v.com/award/
oneshow2004/rec
ID:
04113N

Beyond the Banner
— Single

agency
Modem Media/Norwalk
client
Heineken USA

Writer:
Josh Allen
Producer:
Michael Dwyer
Designers:
Jonathan Damato, Robert Williams
Creative Director:
Mark Galley
URL:
http://awards.modemmedia.com/
eno/04/oneshow/
ID:
04114N

Beyond the Banner
— Single

agency
OgilvyOne worldwide/
London
client
IBM

Art Directors:
Howard Dean, Zak Loney
Writer:
David Shearer
Programmers:
Fraser Campbell, Gary Jobe,
Thorkild Clausen, Peter Lewis-Dale,
Harsha Yogasundrum
Producer:
Rebecca Mackenzie
Designers:
Zak Loney, Howard Dean
Creative Director:
Colin Nimick
URL:
http://www.creative-awards.co.uk/
oneshow03/ibmwimbledon/
ID:
04116N

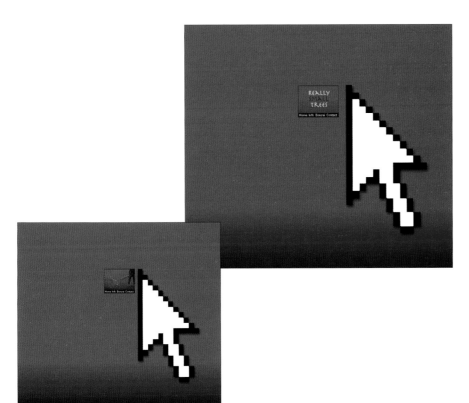

Beyond the Banner — Single

AGENCY
Saatchi & Saatchi/
Frankfurt
CLIENT
Bonsai Rüger

Art Director:
Sebastian Schier
Writer:
Jörn Welle
Producer:
Sebastian Schier
Designers:
Sebastian Schier, Daniel Becker
Information Architect:
Sebastian Schier
Creative Director:
Sebastian Schier
URL:
http://newmedia.saatchi.de/bonsai/eng/
ID:
04117N

Beyond the Banner — Single

AGENCY
SBI.Razorfish/Cambridge
CLIENT
adidas

Art Director:
Aaron Johnsen
Writer:
Carl Vanderzanden
Photographers/Illustrators:
Stan Musilek, Steve Bonini, Todd Eckelman
Programmer:
Ben Brewer
Agency Producers:
Stan Otani, Heather Linn, Rob Shields
Information Architect:
Jonathan Woytek
Creative Director:
Russ Hoffman
URL:
http://usa.adidas.com/tmac
ID:
04148N

Beyond the Banner
— Single

AGENCY
TBWA\Hunt\Lascaris/
Johannesburg
client
BMW Corporate

Art Director:
Theo Ferreira
Writer:
Greg Cohen
Programmer:
Jonathan McKay
Digital Artist/Multimedia:
Jonathan McKay
Agency Producer:
Jo Barber
Production Company:
Tennant McKay
Producer:
Robyn Jephson
Designer:
Tennant McKay
Information Architect:
Greg Cohen
Director:
Jonathan McKay
Creative Directors:
Sue Anderson, Theo Ferreira
URL:
http://www.digerati.co.za/bmw/bixenon/
ID:
04118N

Beyond the Banner
— Single

AGENCY
Venables, Bell & Partners/
San Francisco
client
Napster

Art Director:
Crystal English
Writer:
Quentin Shuldiner
Photographers/Illustrators:
Geoff McFetridge, Ian Kovalik
Agency Producer:
Craig Allen
Production Company:
Mekanism
Producers:
Pete Caban, Stephanie Smith
Designer:
Ian Kovalik
Directors:
Ian Kovalik, Geoff McFetridge
Creative Directors:
Greg Bell, Paul Venables
URL:
http://www.napster.com/bits
ID:
04119N

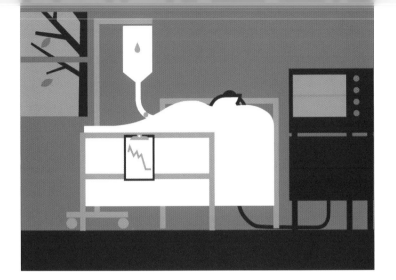

Beyond the Banner
— Single

agency
Venables, Bell & Partners/
San Francisco
client
Napster

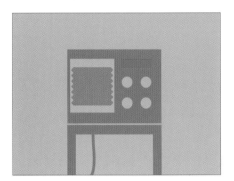

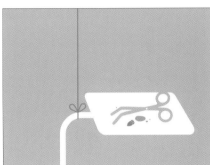

Art Director:
Crystal English
Writers:
Quentin Shuldiner, Matt Rivitz
Photographer/Illustrator:
Geoff McFetridge
Agency Producer:
Craig Allen
Production Company:
Mekanism
Producer:
Pete Caban
Designer:
Ian Kovalik
Director:
Geoff McFetridge, Smashing Ideas
Creative Directors:
Greg Bell, Paul Venables
URL:
http://www.napster.com/bits
ID:
04120N

Beyond the Banner
— Single

agency
Venables, Bell & Partners/
San Francisco
client
Napster

Art Director:
Crystal English
Writers:
Quentin Shuldiner, Matt Rivitz
Photographer/Illustrator:
Geoff McFetridge
Agency Producer:
Craig Allen
Production Company:
Mekanism
Producers:
Pete Caban, Stephanie Smith
Designer:
Ian Kovalik
Director:
Ian Kovalik
Creative Directors:
Greg Bell, Paul Venables
URL:
http://www.napster.com/bits
ID:
04122N

Beyond the Banner
— Single

agency
Venables, Bell & Partners/
San Francisco
client
Napster

Art Director:
Crystal English
Writers:
Quentin Shuldiner, Matt Rivitz
Photographers/Illustrators:
Geoff McFetridge, Ian Kovalik
Agency Producer:
Craig Allen
Production Company:
Mekanism
Producers:
Pete Caban, Stephanie Smith
Designer:
Ian Kovalik
Director:
Ian Kovalik
Creative Directors:
Greg Bell, Paul Venables
URL:
http://www.napster.com/bits
ID:
04123N

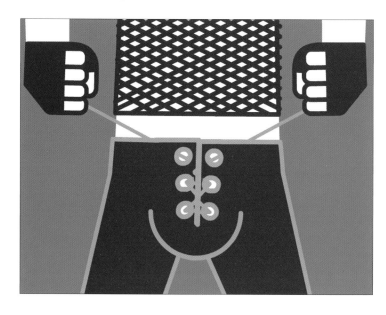

Beyond the Banner
— Single

agency
Venables, Bell & Partners/
San Francisco
client
Napster

Art Director:
Crystal English
Writer:
Quentin Shuldiner
Photographer/Illustrator:
Ian Kovalik
Agency Producer:
Craig Allen
Production Company:
Mekanism
Producer:
Pete Caban
Designer:
Ian Kovalik
Director:
Ian Kovalik
Creative Directors:
Greg Bell, Paul Venables
URL:
http://www.napster.com/bits
ID:
04124N

Beyond the Banner — Single

agency
Zugara/Los Angeles
client
Reebok

Art Director:
Marcus Glover
Writer:
Matthew Szymczyk
Photographers/Illustrators:
Thom Collins, Gary Lamb
Programmers:
Patrik Karolak, Hans Forsman
Agency Producers:
Chad Stoller, Matthew Szymczyk,
Ryan Sills
Production Companies:
Zugara, Reebok, Arnell Group,
Beyond Interactive, FM Rocks
Producer:
Tony Kwan
Designers:
Patrik Karolak, Hans Forsman
Director:
Rawson Marshall Thurber
Creative Directors:
Peter Arnell, Steve Stoute
URL:
http://www.zugara.com/whodunit
ID:
04125N

Beyond the Banner — Campaign

agency
Goodby, Silverstein &
Partners/San Francisco
client
Anheuser-Busch

Art Directors:
Todd Grant, Kris Wixom
Writers:
Steve Dildarian, Alisa Sengel
Photographers/Illustrators:
Steve Dildarian, Kris Wixom
Agency Producer:
James Horner
Information Architect:
Ted DePalma
Creative Directors:
Jeffrey Goodby, Rich Silverstein
URL:
http://www.goodbysilverstein.com/
one_show/spots.html
ID:
04126N

Beyond the Banner
— Campaign

Agency
Goodby, Silverstein &
Partners/San Francisco
client
Anheuser-Busch

Art Directors:
Todd Grant, Kris Wixom
Writers:
Steve Dildarian, Alisa Sengel
Photographers/Illustrators:
Steve Dildarian, Kris Wixom
Agency Producer:
James Horner
Information Architect:
Ted DePalma
Creative Directors:
Jeffrey Goodby, Rich Silverstein
URL:
http://www.goodbysilverstein.com/
one_show/spots.html
ID:
04127N

Beyond the Banner
— Campaign

Agency
Tribal DDB/London
client
Volkswagen

Art Directors:
Sam Ball, Dave Bedwood,
Tim Vance
Writers:
Sam Ball, Dave Bedwood
Programmers:
Dave Cox, Nicole Scholeter,
Nick Clements
Producers:
Sally Gallagher, Robin Grant
Designer:
Tim Vance
Information Architects:
Sam Ball, Dave Bedwood,
Dave Cox
Creative Directors:
Sam Ball, Dave Bedwood
URL:
http://www.tribalddb.co.uk/showcase/
the_touareg_advertising/
ID:
04128N

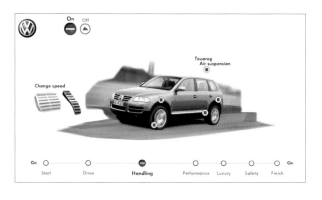

Beyond the Banner
— Campaign

agency
Venables, Bell & Partners/
San Francisco
client
Napster

Art Director:
Crystal English
Writers:
Quentin Shuldiner, Matt Rivitz
Photographers/Illustrators:
Geoff McFetridge, Ian Kovalik
Agency Producer:
Craig Allen
Production Company:
Mekanism
Producer:
Pete Caban
Designers:
Ian Kovalik, Smashing Ideas
Directors:
Geoff McFetridge, Ian Kovalik
Creative Directors:
Greg Bell, Paul Venables
URL:
http://www.napster.com/bits
ID:
04129N

Promotional Advertising
— Web Sites

agency
Aoi Advertising Promotion/
Tokyo
client
SHISEIDO

Art Directors:
Masatoshi Takagi, Kentaro Suda, Rika Hotta
Writer:
Syoko Yoshida
Photographers/Illustrators:
Isao Ito, Seiichi Nakamura, Kaori Hirao
Programmer:
Tomiyoshi Sando
Digital Artist/Multimedia:
Atsuko Uda
Production Companies:
Aoi Advertising Promotion,
RaNa Design Associates
Producers:
Wakako Ishii, Kohta Kanki
Designer:
Yoshie Sumi
Director:
Masato Kanai
Creative Directors:
Katsuhiko Shibuya, Mitsuhisa Aoyama
URL:
http://www.aoi-dc.com/pn-world/html/
ID:
04130N

Promotional Advertising
— Web Sites

Agency
Daiko Advertising/Tokyo
Client
Nike Japan

Art Directors:
Hiroshi Eda, Yasuhito Imai
Writers:
Takuya Sato, Julie Ann Thomas,
Chapter Ten
Photographer/Illustrator:
Tsutomu Umezawa
Digital Artist/Multimedia:
Takeharu Motoki
Agency Producer:
Ryuta Onishi
Production Company:
Aoi Advertising Promotion
Producers:
Shin-ichi Ito, Atsushi Sasaki
Designer:
Yasuhito Imai
Director:
Hiroshi Eda
Creative Directors:
Mitsuhisa Aoyama, Takuya Sato
URL:
http://www.nike.jp/acg/
tumalo/air_tumalo.html
ID:
04133N

Promotional Advertising
— Web Sites

Agency
Daiko Advertising/Tokyo
Client
Nike Japan

Art Director:
Shinji Nemoto
Writer:
Takuya Sato
Photographer/Illustrator:
Jun Tsuzuki
Programmer:
Shinji Nemoto
Production Company:
nem + Tsuzuki
Producer:
Ryuta Onishi
Designer:
Shinji Nemoto
Creative Directors:
Takuya Sato, Hideyuki Arihuku
URL:
http://www.nneemm.com/
play-e/play.html
ID:
04134N

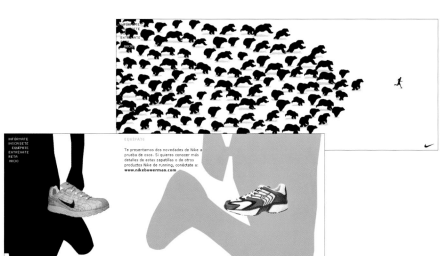

Promotional Advertising — Web Sites

AGENCY
DoubleYou/Barcelona
CLIENT
American Nike

Art Directors:
Anna Coll, Quim Tarrida
Writers:
Eduard Pou, Joakim Borgström,
Oriol Villar
Programmers:
Josep Maria Soler, Joakim Borgström,
Jose Rubio
Digital Artists/Multimedia:
Mauricio Mazzariol, Ale Bica
Producer:
Jordi Pont
Designer:
Elisabeth Badía
Information Architects:
Antonio Buenosvinos, Álvaro Sandoval
Creative Directors:
Eduard Pou, Joakim Borgström,
Oriol Villar
URL:
http://www.doubleyou.com/festivals/
nikesansilvestre/oneshow.html
ID:
04135N

Promotional Advertising — Web Sites

AGENCY
Euro RSCG 4D/New York
CLIENT
Volvo Cars

Art Directors:
Adam Jackson, Bruce Doescher,
Jeff Prybosky
Writers:
Brian Wright, Heather Martin
Programmer:
Gabe Garner
Producers:
Heather Martin, Daissy Vicuna
Creative Director:
Arthur Ceria
URL:
http://www.allnews40.com/
ID:
04136N

Promotional Advertising — Web Sites

Agency
Fort Franklin/Boston
client
ESPN

Art Directors:
Eric Sutton, Marc Gallucci
Writer:
Pete Shamon
Photographers/Illustrators:
Stock, Eric Sutton
Programmers:
Eric Sutton, Platform 360
Digital Artist/Multimedia:
Eric Sutton
Designers:
Eric Sutton, Brandun Kayal
Creative Director:
Marc Gallucci
URL:
http://www.espnstanleycupgames.com
ID:
04137N

Promotional Advertising — Web Sites

Agency
Genex/Culver City
client
American Honda Motor
Company/Acura Division

Art Director:
Wilson Yin
Writer:
Theo Wallace
Photographers/Illustrators:
John Early, Wilson Yin
Programmer:
Ryan Hunt
Digital Artists/Multimedia:
Wilson Yin, Alan Gilles,
Peter Boerboom, Daniel Alegria
Producer:
Jim DeRosa
Designer:
Wilson Yin
Creative Directors:
David Glaze, Ron Spohn
URL:
http://www.acura.com/
tlshowroombiscuit
ID:
04138N

Promotional Advertising
— Web Sites

AGENCY
henderson bas/Toronto
CLIENT
Nike Canada

Art Director:
Stephen Bennett
Writers:
Jon Finkelstein, Bill James
Programmers:
Guande Wang, Jeff Sangster, Boris Pan,
Suzanne Johnson, Andrew White
Digital Artists/Multimedia:
Allan Kennedy, Davin Risk
Producers:
Jeremey Weinstein, Duane Currie,
Andrew Chow
Designers:
Paul McDougall, Stephen Bennett,
David Wilson, Phil Bonnell
Information Architect:
Scott Duncan
Creative Director:
Jon Finkelstein
URL:
http://nikedevelopmentdynamo.yyz.ninedots.
com/nikedevelopment/canada/runto1
ID:
04144N

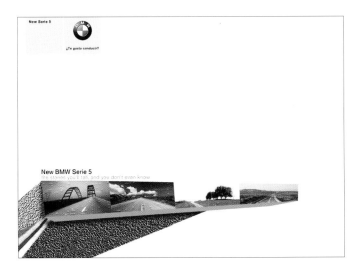

Promotional Advertising
— Web Sites

AGENCY
Herraiz Soto & Co./
Barcelona
CLIENT
BMW

Art Directors:
Angel Herraiz, Sergi Mula
Writer:
Rafa Soto
Programmers:
Carles Sanz, Genis Bayarri
Creative Directors:
Angel Herraiz, Rafa Soto
URL:
http://www.herraizsoto.com/
festivales/serie5web
ID:
04139N

Promotional Advertising
— Web Sites

agency
Hi-ReS!/London
client
Artisan Entertainment/
Lions Gate

Art Directors:
Florian Schmitt, Alexandra Jugovic
Writer:
Dave Stern
Programmers:
Andreas Müller, Tommi Eberwein,
Florian Schmitt, Marc Kremers, Bela Spahn
Digital Artists/Multimedia:
Florian Schmitt, Alexandra Jugovic,
Marc Kremers, Tommi Eberwein
Producers:
Paul David, Artisan/Lions Gate
Designers:
Florian Schmitt, Alexandra Jugovic,
Marc Kremers, Tommi Eberwein
Creative Directors:
Florian Schmitt, Alexandra Jugovic
URL:
http://www.punisherthemovie.com/
ID:
04140N

Promotional Advertising
— Web Sites

agency
Hi-ReS!/London
client
HBO/New York

Art Directors:
Alexandra Jugovic, Florian Schmitt
Writers:
Matthew Anderson, Dan Sacher,
Cara DiPaolo, Joanna Lovinger
Programmers:
Bela Spahn, Andreas Müller
Digital Artists/Multimedia:
Alexandra Jugovic, Florian Schmitt,
Erik Jarlsson
Producers:
Matthew Anderson, Dan Sacher
Designers:
Alexandra Jugovic, Florian Schmitt,
Erik Jarlsson
Creative Directors:
Alexandra Jugovic, Florian Schmitt
URL:
http://www.hbo.com/sixfeetunder/swf/
wake/moment2003/wake2003.html
ID:
04141N

Promotional Advertising
— Web Sites

Agency
J. Walter Thompson/Detroit
Client
Ford Motor Company

Art Directors:
Nicholas D'Angelo, Ken Tadeo
Writer:
Randy Campbell
Digital Artists/Multimedia:
Justin Mysza, Shane Mielke
Agency Producer:
Kim Blommer
Producer:
Samantha Burton
Designer:
Kevin McElroy
Information Architect:
Patrick Callow
Creative Directors:
Tom Cordner, Dave Garant,
Ken Tadeo
URL:
http://www.fordvehicles.com/
trucks/f-150
ID:
04143N

Promotional Advertising
— Web Sites

Agency
Nordpol/Hamburg
Client
ASICS Europe

Art Director:
Gunther Schreiber
Writer:
Ingmar Bartels
Designers:
Dominik Anweiler, Mark Hoefler
Creative Director:
Ingo Fritz
URL:
http://www.asicsmarathon.com
ID:
04145N

Promotional Advertising
— Web Sites

agency
OgilvyInteractive worldwide/
New York
client
IBM

Art Director:
Cynthia Dauzier
Writer:
Jay Zasa
Digital Artist/Multimedia:
Heavy
Producer:
Solange Claudio
Information Architect:
Paul Caron
Creative Director:
Greg Kaplan
URL:
http://www.wwpl.net/oneshow2004/
ibm/prodigy.html
ID:
04199N

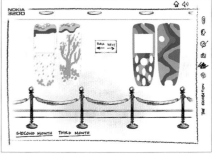

Promotional Advertising
— Web Sites

agency
OgilvyOne worldwide/
Singapore
client
Nokia

Art Director:
Ashidiq Ghazali
Writer:
Audra Tan
Programmers:
Chandra Barathi, Colin Foo, Raju TV
Producer:
Memi Chang
Designer:
Arnold Widjanarko
Creative Director:
Dominic Goldman
URL:
http://www.our-work.com/nokia/3200/
ID:
04146N

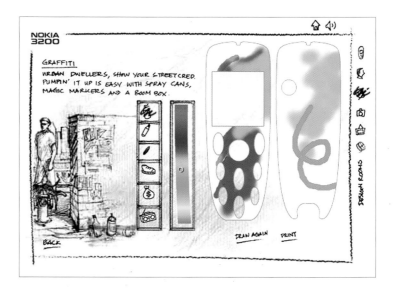

Promotional Advertising — Web Sites

agency
SarkissianlMason/New York
client
Mazda North
American Operations

Programmer:
Ben Ursu
Producer:
Marybeth Atzinger
Designers:
Dale Castro, Rick Snailem,
Andy Gray
Director:
Patrick Sarkissian
Creative Director:
Matt Mason
URL:
http://www.mazdausa.com/MusaWeb/
rx8/xmen/rx8_xmen_flash.jsp
ID:
04147N

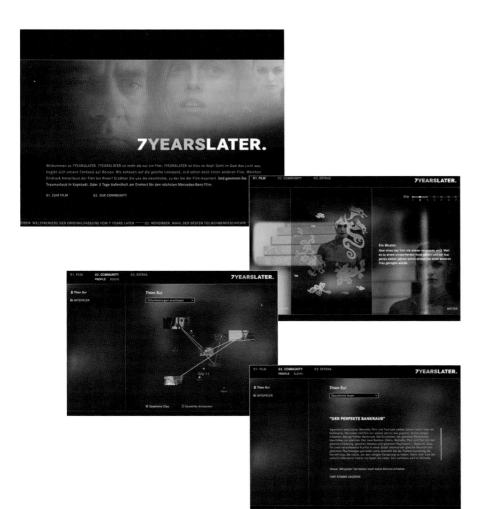

Promotional Advertising — Web Sites

agency
Scholz & Volkmer/Wiesbaden
client
Mercedes-Benz

Writer:
Andreas Henke
Programmers:
Duc-Thuan Bui, Thorsten Kraus
Designer:
Jenny Fitz
Information Architect:
Christoph Kehren
Creative Director:
Heike Brockmann
URL:
http://www.mercedes-benz.com/
7yearslater
ID:
04149N

Promotional Advertising
— Web Sites

agency
Wunderman Interactive/
London
client
Ford

Art Director:
Richard Last
Writer:
Iain Harrison
Programmer:
Simon Jones
Digital Artist/Multimedia:
Richard Barrett
Producers:
Danna Barden, Rishi Ramjotton
Designer:
Richard Barrett
Information Architects:
Mark Plant, Paul Rasmussen
Creative Director:
Simon Milliship
URL:
http://www.the-eviltwin.co.uk
ID:
04150N

Promotional Advertising
— Web Sites

agency
Wysiwyg Comunicacion
Interactiva/Madrid
client
Saez Merino

Art Director:
Marga Castaño
Writer:
Esther de la Rosa
Programmer:
Raúl Ortega
Producer:
Victor Madueño
Creative Director:
Adolfo González Vicente
URL:
http://www.wysiwyg.net/festivals2004/
cimarron
ID:
04151N

Promotional Advertising — CD-ROMs

Agency
Tribal DDB/Ultimo
Client
Norman Disney Young

Art Director:
Heath Rudduck
Writer:
David Pisker
Photographers/Illustrators:
Stuart Campbell, Heath Rudduck, Mike Tan
Programmers:
Stuart Campbell, Mike Tan
Digital Artists/Multimedia:
Stuart Campbell, Heath Rudduck, Mike Tan
Producer:
David Pisker
Designers:
Heath Rudduck, Stuart Campbell
Information Architect:
David Pisker
Creative Director:
Heath Rudduck
ID:
04152N

Promotional Advertising — CD-ROMs

Agency
Tribal DDB/Ultimo
Client
Volkswagen Group Australia

Art Director:
Mark Cracknell
Writer:
Trevor Crossman
Photographer/Illustrator:
Mark Cracknell
Programmer:
Mark Cracknell
Digital Artist/Multimedia:
Mark Cracknell
Producer:
Mike Boyd
Designer:
Ivan Yip
Creative Director:
Mark Cracknell
ID:
04153N

Promotional Advertising
— Other Digital Media

Agency
Hill, Holliday, Connors,
Cosmopulos/Boston
Client
Thermo Electron

Art Director:
Darryl Jelley
Writer:
Brian Cleary
Photographer/Illustrator:
Raoul Kim
Programmer:
Filio
Digital Artist/Multimedia:
Thibault Kim
Designers:
Sean Mahoney, Thibault Kim
Creative Director:
Darryl Jelley
ID:
04154N

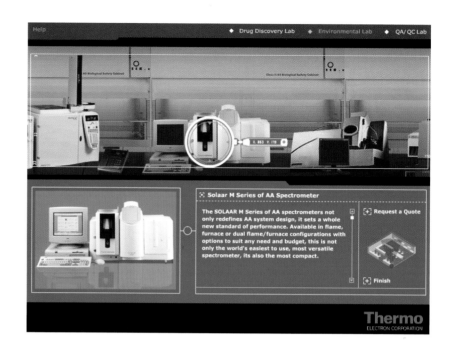

Promotional Advertising
— Other Digital Media

Agency
IQ television group/Atlanta
Client
National Geographic

Art Director:
IQ television group
Writer:
IQ television group
Programmer:
IQ television group
Creative Director:
IQ television group
URL:
http://www.iqtv.com/portfolio/
natgeoALT/
ID:
04155N

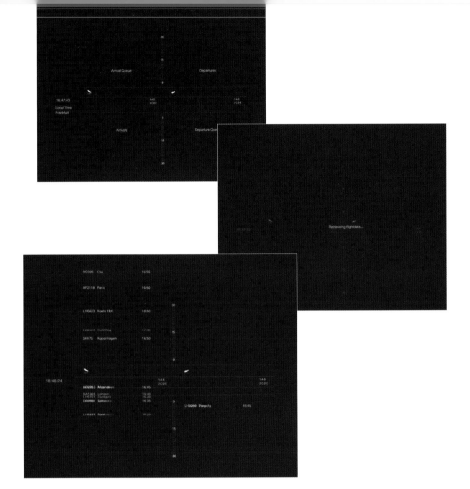

Promotional Advertising
— Other Digital Media

agency
Scholz & Volkmer/Wiesbaden
client
Fraport AG

Art Director:
Anne Wichmann
Programmer:
Peter Reichard
Information Architects:
Rainer Eidemüller, Peter Reichard,
Michael Volkmer
Creative Director:
Michael Volkmer
URL:
http://www.s-v.de/projects/fraport
ID:
04156N

Promotional Advertising
— Other Digital Media

agency
TBWA\London
client
TBWA\London

Art Director:
Steve Williams
Writer:
Simon Hardy
Agency Producer:
Diane Croll
Production Company:
Stark
Director:
Simon Cracknell
Creative Director:
Trevor Beattie
ID:
04157N

Also Awarded
Merit:
Corporate Image B2B – Other Digital Media
Merit:
Self-Promotion – Other Digital Media

Corporate Image B2C — Web Sites

Agency
The Barbarian Group/
Boston

Client
Nike ACG

Art Director:
The Barbarian Group
Writer:
The Barbarian Group
Programmer:
The Barbarian Group
Creative Director:
The Barbarian Group
URL:
http://www.nikeacg.com
ID:
04185N

Corporate Image B2C — Web Sites

Agency
BBDO InterOne/Hamburg

Client
BMW AG

Art Director:
Johannes Faeth
Writers:
Jan-Hendrik Simons, Rachel McLaughlin,
Muriel Fuchs
Programmers:
Nicole Kengyel, Soeren Jatho,
Rico Marquardt, Henning Boeger
Digital Artists/Multimedia:
Wolfgang Mueller, Matthias Mach
Producers:
Eric Funk, Holger Nauen
Designers:
Rassul Wassa, Birgit Rohde,
Melanie Schultze-Breitsprecher
Creative Directors:
Jan-Hendrik Simons, Johannes Faeth
URL:
http://www.bmw.com/x3
ID:
04158N

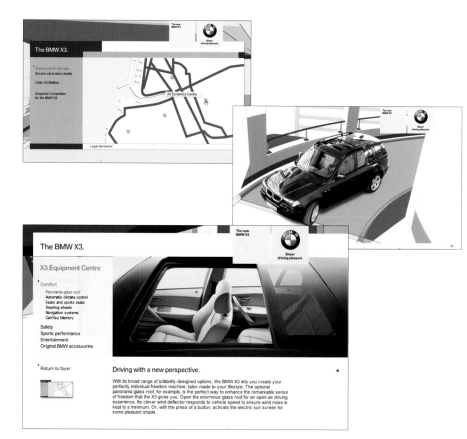

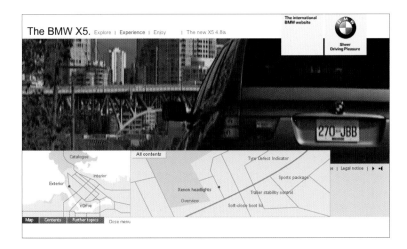

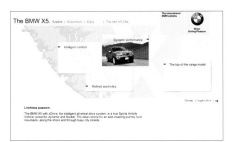

Corporate Image B2C — Web Sites

Agency
BBDO InterOne/Hamburg
Client
BMW AG

Art Director:
Regina Buss
Writers:
Patrick Fonger, Jonathan Long,
Muriel Fuchs
Programmer:
Christian Nordwald
Digital Artists/Multimedia:
Jan Mankopf, Torben Cording,
David Hoffmann
Producers:
Roland Aust, Eric Funk
Designers:
Carmen Krueger, Olaf Boquist
Creative Director:
Nathalie Zimmermann
URL:
http://www.bmw.com/x5
ID:
04159N

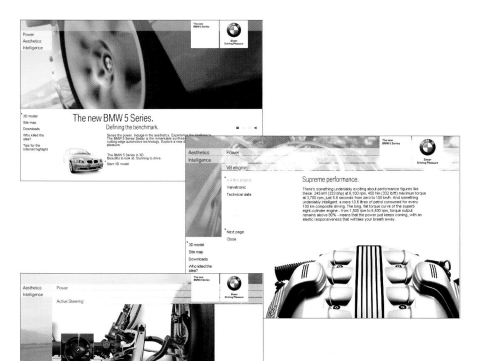

Corporate Image B2C — Web Sites

Agency
BBDO InterOne/Hamburg
Client
BMW AG

Art Director:
Sven Loskill
Writers:
Jan-Hendrik Simons, Matthias Schaefer,
Rachel McLaughlin, Muriel Fuchs
Programmers:
Marc Hitzmann, Sven Loskill,
Wolfgang Mueller
Producer:
Roland Aust
Creative Director:
Hannes Schmidt
URL:
http://www.bmw.com/5series
ID:
04160N

Corporate Image B2C
— Web Sites

Agency
BBDO InterOne/Hamburg
Client
BMW AG

Writers:
Jan-Hendrik Simons, Muriel Fuchs,
Jonathan Long, Sharon Moody
Programmers:
Werner Rauch, Marc Hitzmann
Digital Artist/Multimedia:
Greg Jacobs
Designers:
Regina Buss, Felix Genzmer
Creative Director:
Nathalie Zimmermann
URL:
http://www.bmw.com/6seriesconvertible
ID:
04161N

Corporate Image B2C
— Web Sites

Agency
Blast Radius/Vancouver
Client
BMW Group Canada

Art Directors:
Mark Wallace, Michael Oliver
Writer:
Wendy Schaffer
Programmers:
Anthony Toric, Brendan Lynch,
Joseph Nittoly, Dan Truong,
Marsette Apilado
Production Company:
Blast Radius
Producers:
Christine Pilkington, Kevin Jones
Designers:
Michael Oliver, Tristan Spence,
Francis Chan, Mark Abernathy
Information Architect:
Lisa Fitzgerald
Creative Directors:
Mark Wallace, Peter Hong,
Elizabeth Kis
URL:
http://www.mini.ca
ID:
04162N

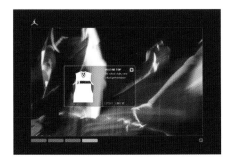

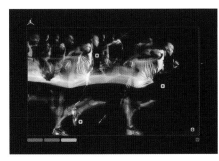

Corporate Image B2C — Web Sites

agency
Blast Radius/Vancouver
client
Jordan Brand

Art Director:
Marcus Ericsson
Writer:
Greg Liburd
Programmers:
Steve Bond, Rodrigo Gomez-Tagle,
Jean-Noel Filippi, Terrance Yu,
Rene Gourley
Digital Artist/Multimedia:
Patrick Redding
Agency Producer:
Michael Smit
Production Company:
Blast Radius
Producer:
William Azaroff
Designers:
Hannes Ottahal, Aimee Croteau
Creative Director:
Jon Maltby
URL:
http://www.nike.com/jumpman23/
features/mj/
ID:
04163N

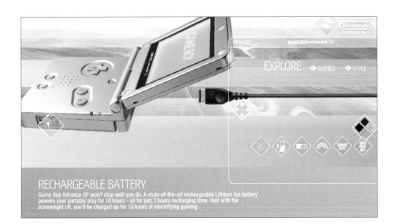

Corporate Image B2C — Web Sites

agency
Blast Radius/Vancouver
client
Nintendo of Europe

Art Directors:
Remon Tijssen, Folkert Gorter
Writers:
Mark Green (Nintendo of Europe),
Richard Moulton (Nintendo of Europe)
Programmer:
Shaun Krislock
Production Company:
Blast Radius
Producer:
Erin Cooper
Creative Director:
Lee Feldman
URL:
http://www.nintendo-europe.com/
gameboyadvancesp
ID:
04164N

Corporate Image B2C
— Web Sites

agency
Business Architects/Tokyo
client
K. Mikimoto & Co.

Art Directors:
Shinzo Fukui, Yosuke Abe
Writer:
Muneki Shimizu
Photographer/Illustrator:
Koichiro Doi
Programmers:
Eiji Muroichi, Toshinari Yanagisawa,
Ryuji Sakai
Producer:
Maiko Hotta
Designers:
Daisuke Horiuchi, Yasuhiko Kuroda,
Kinya Masuo
Information Architect:
Miwa Ichijo
Creative Director:
Shinzo Fukui
URL:
http://www.mikimoto.com/
ID:
04165N

Corporate Image B2C
— Web Sites

agency
Business Architects/Tokyo
client
Mori Building

Art Directors:
Tomonari Ogino, Yugo Nakamura
Programmer:
Koichi Kaneda
Producer:
Maiko Hotta
Designer:
Tomonari Ogino
Creative Director:
Shinzo Fukui
URL:
http://www.moriartscenter.org/
en/index.html
ID:
04166N

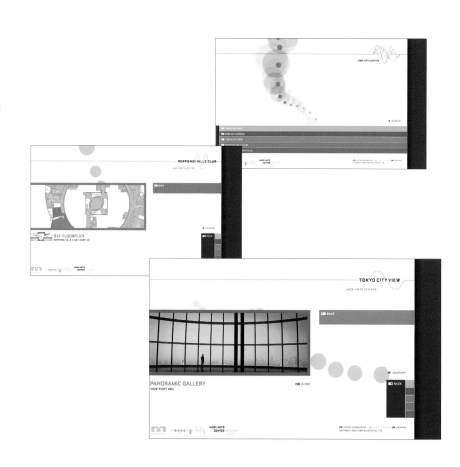

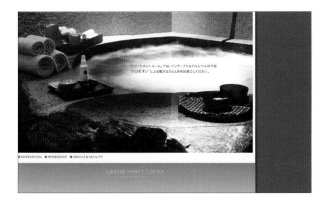

Corporate Image B2C
— Web Sites

agency
Business Architects/Tokyo
client
Mori Hospitality
Corporation

Art Directors:
Shinzo Fukui, Tomonari Ogino
Programmer:
Eiji Muroichi
Producer:
Maiko Hotta
Designer:
Tomonari Ogino
Creative Director:
Shinzo Fukui
URL:
http://www.grandhyatttokyo.com/
ID:
04167N

Corporate Image B2C
— Web Sites

agency
Firstborn Multimedia/
New York
client
Victoria's Secret

Programmers:
Josh Ott, Gicheol Lee
Production Company:
Firstborn Multimedia
Producer:
Jeremy Berg
Designer:
Vas Sloutchevsky
Information Architect:
Vas Sloutchevsky
Creative Director:
Vas Sloutchevsky
URL:
http://www.firstbornmultimedia.com/
websites/081_vs_bluelondon
ID:
04168N

Corporate Image B2C
— Web Sites

AGENCY
Framfab/Copenhagen
CLIENT
Carlsberg

Art Directors:
Lars Cortsen, Damian Claassens
Writers:
Thomas Robson, Lewis Raven,
Lars Bastholm
Progammers:
Kåre Wesnæs, Philip Louderback
Producers:
Mikala Remvig, Lotte Ronan
Designers:
Damian Claassens, Patrick Danielsson,
Anders Gramkow
Information Architect:
Andreas Iversen
Creative Director:
Lars Bastholm
URL:
http://www.carlsberg.com
ID:
04169N

Corporate Image B2C
— Web Sites

AGENCY
Framfab/Copenhagen
CLIENT
Nike Europe

Art Director:
Rasmus Frandsen
Writer:
Lewis Raven
Programmer:
Jesper Arvidson
Digital Artist/Multimedia:
Anders Gustafsson
Producer:
Caroline Bendixen
Information Architect:
Jens Christiansen
Creative Director:
Lars Bastholm
URL:
http://www.nikefootball.com
ID:
04170N

Corporate Image B2C
— Web Sites

Agency
Framfab/Copenhagen
Client
Nike Europe

Art Director:
Lars Cortsen
Writer:
Rhiannon Davies
Programmers:
Kim Jensen, Brian Dickens
Digital Artist/Multimedia:
Peter Ringtved
Producers:
Sara Trier, Marie Baltzersen
Designer:
Robert Thomsen
Information Architect:
Andreas Iversen
Creative Director:
Lars Bastholm
URL:
http://www.nikewomen.com
ID:
04171N

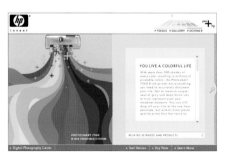

Corporate Image B2C
— Web Sites

Agency
Goodby, Silverstein &
Partners/San Francisco
Client
Hewlett-Packard

Art Director:
Milena Sadee
Writer:
Aaron Griffiths
Production Company:
WDDG
Producer:
Amanda Kelso
Information Architect:
Carrie Whitehead
Creative Directors:
Steve Simpson, Keith Anderson
URL:
http://www.hp.com/you
ID:
04172N

Corporate Image B2C
— Web Sites

Agency
Jung von Matt/Hamburg
Client
ONe-the functional drink

Art Director:
Elke Klinkhammer
Writer:
Friedrich von Zitzewitz
Photographer/Illustrator:
Sergei Juaney
Programmers:
Andre Wischenwski, Daniel Mautz
Producers:
Marc Seibert, Marijana Kélava
Designer:
Christoph Behm
Creative Director:
Michael Kutschinski
URL:
http://award.jvm.de/en/one/
ID:
04173N

Corporate Image B2C
— Web Sites

Agency
Kinetic Interactive/
Singapore
Client
KAH Motor Singapore

Art Director:
Sean Lam
Writer:
Alex Goh
Photographer/Illustrator:
Sean Lam
Programmer:
Sean Lam
Producers:
Matthew Quah, Adeline Tan
Designer:
Sean Lam
Information Architect:
Sean Lam
Creative Director:
Kinetic Interactive
URL:
http://www.honda.com.sg/main.htm
ID:
04174N

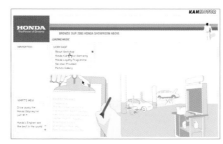

Corporate Image B2C
— Web Sites

Agency
Lateral/London
client
Levi's Europe

Art Director:
Simon Crab
Writer:
David Jones
Programmers:
Karsten Schmidt, NeoWorks
Digital Artist/Multimedia:
Rob Gibson
Producer:
Daniel Bambach
Designers:
Sam Collett, Ted Hunt, Laura Jordan,
Mark Hanlon
Information Architect:
Daniel Bambach
Director:
Jon Bains
Creative Director:
Simon Crab
URL:
http://twotwisted.lateral.net/
ID:
04175N

Corporate Image B2C
— Web Sites

Agency
Neue Digitale/
Frankfurt am Main
client
adidas-Salomon AG

Art Director:
Rolf Borcherding
Writer:
Roland Grossmann
Programmers:
Jens Steffen, Marius Bulla
Creative Director:
Olaf Czeschner
URL:
http://www.neue-digitale.de/
awards/y3.html
ID:
04176N

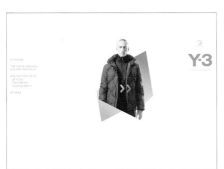

Corporate Image B2C
— Web Sites

agency
OgilvyOne worldwide/
Singapore
client
Levi Strauss

Art Directors:
Ashidiq Ghazali, Dominic Goldman
Writer:
Audra Tan
Programmers:
Chandra Barathi, Dara Lim, Colin Foo,
Raju TV, Ronnie Liew
Producer:
Yow Pin Fern
Designers:
Ashidiq Ghazali, Dominic Goldman,
Arnold Widjanarko
Creative Director:
Dominic Goldman
URL:
http://www.our-work.com/
levis/site/index_main.html
ID:
04177N

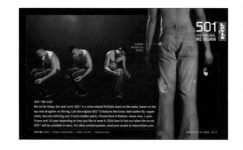

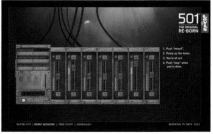

Corporate Image B2C
— Web Sites

agency
Organic/Bloomfield Hills
client
Reebok

Art Director:
Brian Carley
Writer:
Michael Barnwell
Producers:
Esteban González, Jason Wulkowicz
Designers:
Shu Hung, Joseph Magliaro
Creative Director:
Justin Crawford
URL:
http://www.reebok.com/x/
us/vector/features/tech/
ID:
04178N

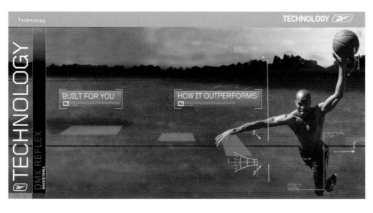

Corporate Image B2C — Web Sites

Agency
Platinum Design/New York
Client
John Kenney And

Programmer:
Jonathan Hammer
Designer:
Andrew Taray
Creative Director:
Vickie Peslak
URL:
http://www.jkand.com
ID:
04179N

Corporate Image B2C — Web Sites

Agency
Pop & Co./New York
Client
LEGO

Art Director:
Jesse McGowan
Photographer/Illustrator:
Scott Gursky
Producers:
Kelly Galligan, Demetri Detsaridis
Designer:
Scott Gursky
Information Architect:
Frank Lantz
Creative Director:
Vincent Lacava
URL:
http://www.popandco.com/
archive/moab
ID:
04180N

Corporate Image B2C — Web Sites

AGENCY
R/GA/New York
CLIENT
Nike

Art Director:
Nathan Iverson
Writer:
Jason Marks
Programmers:
Chuck Genco, Charles Duncan
Producer:
Shawn Natko
Designers:
Andrew Hsu, David Morrow
Information Architect:
Richard Ting
URL:
http://www.nikebasketball.com
ID:
04181N

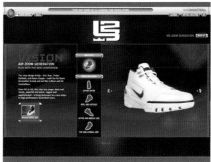

Corporate Image B2C — Web Sites

AGENCY
R/GA/New York
CLIENT
Nike

Art Directors:
Nathan Iverson, Rei Inamoto
Writers:
Jason Marks, Ken Hamm,
Andrew Kessler
Programmers:
Lucas Shuman, Stan Weichers,
Hamid Younessi, Scott Prindle
Digital Artists/Multimedia:
Stephen Barnwell, Matt Walsh
Producer:
Beverly May
Designers:
Misha Gervitz, Sacha Sedriks
Information Architects:
Pat Stern, Kip Voytek,
Matt Walsh
Creative Director:
Rei Inamoto
URL:
http://www.nikegridiron.com
ID:
04182N

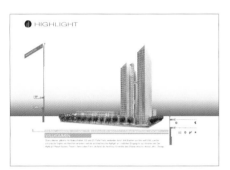

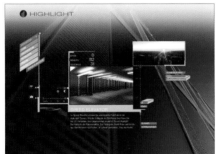

Corporate Image B2C — Web Sites

agency
Scholz & Volkmer/
Wiesbaden
client
Bürozentrum Parkstadt
München-Schwabing KG

Art Director:
Katja Rickert
Writers:
Carsten Fillinger, Chris Kohl
Programmers:
Duc-Thuan Bui, Philipp Just,
Thorsten Kraus
Designers:
Katja Rickert, Elke Nied
Information Architects:
Duc-Thuan Bui, Thorsten Kraus,
Katja Rickert, Sabine Schmidt
URL:
http://www.highlight-towers.com
ID:
04183N

Corporate Image B2C — Web Sites

agency
Scholz & Volkmer/
Wiesbaden
client
Ingo Maurer

Art Directors:
Jörg Waldschütz, Christa Heinold
Programmers:
Natasha Becker, Sebastian Klein,
Mario Dold, Jan Schlag
Designers:
Jörg Waldschütz, Christa Heinold,
Marion Stolz
Information Architects:
Christoph Kehren, Jörg Waldschütz,
Christa Heinold
Creative Director:
Anette Scholz
URL:
http://www.ingo-maurer.com
ID:
04184N

Corporate Image B2C
— Web Sites

agency
Wysiwyg Comunicacion
Interactiva/Madrid
client
Camper

Art Director:
Pablo Martín
Writer:
Cristina Barchi
Programmers:
Victor Madueño, Raúl Ortega
Digital Artist/Multimedia:
Marga Castaño
Producer:
Janina Bea
Designer:
Gráfica
Information Architect:
Javier Batanero
Creative Director:
Shubhankar Ray
URL:
http://www.wysiwyg.net/
festivals2004/tw6
ID:
04186N

Corporate Image B2C
— CD-ROMs

agency
IA Collaborative/Chicago
client
Nike

Art Director:
Dan Kraemer
Writers:
Jason Eplawy, Ted Helprin
Photographers/Illustrators:
Jason Eplawy, Chris von Ende
Producer:
Ted Helprin
Designer:
Jason Eplawy
Information Architect:
Kathleen Bradenburg
ID:
04187N

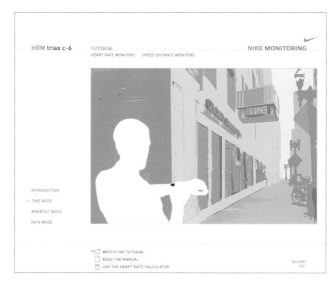

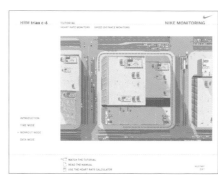

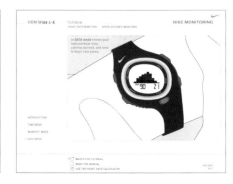

Corporate Image B2C — CD-ROMs

Agency
IA Collaborative/Chicago
Client
Nike

Art Directors:
Jason Eplawy, Dan Kraemer
Writers:
Jason Eplawy, Ted Helprin
Photographer/Illustrator:
Ross Forbes
Programmers:
Russ Forbes, Ryan Rehal
Producer:
Ted Helprin
Designers:
Jason Eplawy, Russ Forbes,
Chris von Ende
Information Architects:
Jason Eplawy, Chris von Ende
ID:
04188N

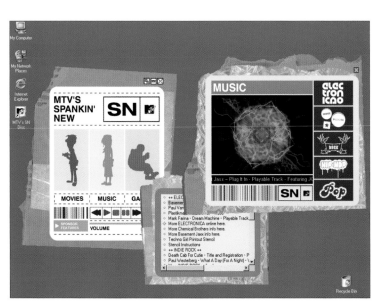

Corporate Image B2C — CD-ROMs

Agency
MTV Networks/New York
Client
MTV

Art Director:
Andrew Lopez
Writers:
Ken Saji, Patrick O'Sullivan,
Marina Khidekel
Programmer:
Patrick Snell
Digital Artists/Multimedia:
Richard Tancin, Thaddeus Rombauer
Agency Producer:
MTV Networks Creative Services
Producers:
Alan Perler, Mark Malabrigo
Designer:
Andrew Lopez
Information Architect:
Richard Tancin
Creative Directors:
Scott Wadler, Cheryl Family
ID:
04189N

agency
Bartle Bogle Hegarty/
New York
client
Unilever/
Axe Essence

Art Director:
Gerald Lewis
Writer:
Matt Ian
Agency Producer:
Melissa Bemis
Production Company:
Biscuit Films
Designer:
Matt Campbell
Director:
Jeffery Fleisig
Creative Director:
William Gelner
URL:
http://www.theaxeeffect.com/
essence
ID:
04190N

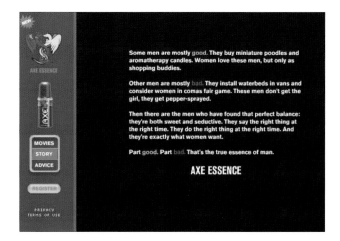

agency
Herraiz Soto & Co./
Barcelona
client
Mahou

Art Director:
Andreu Colomer
Writer:
Rafa Soto
Programmers:
Javier Alvarez, Arnau Bosch
Producer:
Ovideo
Designer:
Albert Corberó
Creative Directors:
Angel Herraiz, Rafa Soto
URL:
http://www.herraizsoto.com/
festivales/nosepuede
ID:
04191N

Corporate Image B2B
— Web Sites

agency
Arteaga Interactivo/
San Juan
client
Air Master

Art Director:
Ramón Reyes
Writer:
Odaly Santiago
Programmers:
Ramón Reyes, David Sanchez
Digital Artists/Multimedia:
Gabriela Lopez, Ramón Reyes
Designers:
Gabriela Lopez, Ramón Reyes
Information Architects:
Ramón Reyes, Odaly Santiago
URL:
http://www.airmasterpr.com
ID:
04192N

Corporate Image B2B
— Web Sites

agency
cosmoblonde/Berlin
client
Bacardi

Art Director:
Michael Scholz
Writer:
catfish creative
Programmers:
Heiko Milke, Thomas Bethe
Digital Artists/Multimedia:
Martin Missfeldt, Thomas Laubner
Production Company:
cosmoblonde
Producers:
Christina Kempe, Anjana Muschenich
Designers:
Junia Keutel, Monic Meisel
Information Architect:
Frank Wulf
Creative Directors:
Anjana Muschenich, Michael Scholz
URL:
http://www.bacardi-deutschland.de
ID:
04193N

Corporate Image B2B — Web Sites

Agency
Hillmancurtis/New York
client
Sideshow Creative

Art Directors:
Michel Suissa, Hillman Curtis
Writer:
Candace Reid
Photographer/Illustrator:
Hillman Curtis
Programmers:
Hillman Curtis, Gabe Garner
Digital Artist/Multimedia:
Hillman Curtis
Producer:
Michael Pollock
Designer:
Hillman Curtis
Information Architect:
Hillman Curtis
Creative Directors:
Hillman Curtis, Michel Suissa
URL:
http://www.hillmancurtis.com/
contest
ID:
04194N

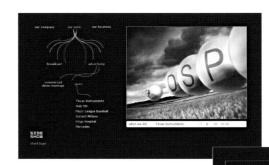

Corporate Image B2B — Web Sites

Agency
IconNicholson/New York
client
EMI Music Publishing

Art Director:
See-ming Lee
Programmers:
Jason Wurtzel, Tim Murtaugh
Digital Artist/Multimedia:
Yun Rhee
Producer:
Marshall Curry
Designers:
Claudia Chow, Chris Brugh
Information Architects:
Jeff Salem, Zeina Farha
Creative Director:
Matt Berninger
URL:
http://www.emimusicpub.com
ID:
04195N

Corporate Image B2B — Web Sites

Agency
Jung von Matt/Stuttgart
Client
IFB Dr. Braschel AG

Art Director:
Stefan Walz
Writers:
Peter Waibel, Matthias Kubitz
Programmers:
Holger Prys, Stefanie Welker
Agency Producer:
Dorothea Feurer
Designer:
Stefan Walz
Creative Director:
Achim Jäger
URL:
http://www.ifb.de
ID:
04196N

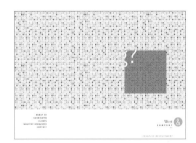

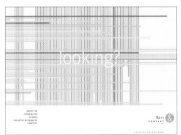

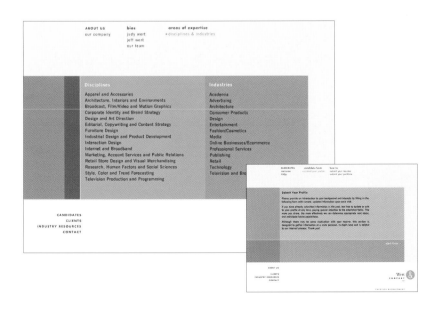

Corporate Image B2B — Web Sites

Agency
Nick Law/Knoxville
Client
Wert & Company

Art Director:
Nick Law
Programmers:
Marlon Hernandez, Noah Landow,
Joseph Aulisi, Peter Norton,
Mark Munro
Designers:
Nick Law, Marlon Hernandez
Information Architect:
Nick Law
Creative Director:
Nick Law
URL:
http://www.wertco.com
ID:
04197N

Corporate Image B2B
— Web Sites

Agency
OgilvyInteractive worldwide/
São Paulo
Client
IBM

Art Director:
Milton Correa Jr.
Writer:
Moacyr Guimarães Netto
Programmers:
Vincent Maraschin, Henrique Romero
Designers:
Milton Correa Jr., Felipe Mahalem,
André Attanasio
Creative Directors:
Adriana Cury, Paulo Sanna
URL:
http://www.ogilvy.com.br/
ourwork2004/simulator
ID:
04198N

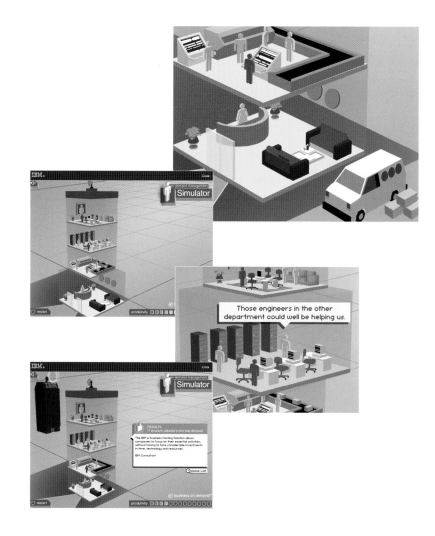

Corporate Image B2B
— Web Sites

Agency
Saatchi & Saatchi/London
Client
Saatchi & Saatchi

Art Director:
Tony Snow
Writer:
Robin England
Programmer:
Tom Eslinger
Agency Producer:
Norma Clarke
Producer:
Lara Bowen
Designer:
Tom Eslinger
Creative Director:
Trefor Thomas
URL:
http://www.saatchi.com
ID:
04200N

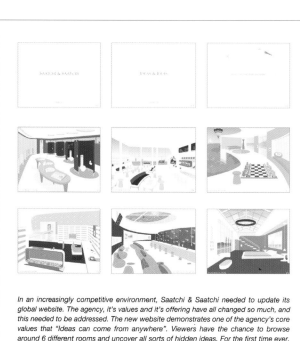

In an increasingly competitive environment, Saatchi & Saatchi needed to update its global website. The agency, it's values and it's offering have all changed so much, and this needed to be addressed. The new website demonstrates one of the agency's core values that "Ideas can come from anywhere". Viewers have the chance to browse around 6 different rooms and uncover all sorts of hidden ideas. For the first time ever, the global website also showcases some of the agency's work, allowing prospective clients the chance to see what the network is producing, both currently and in the past.

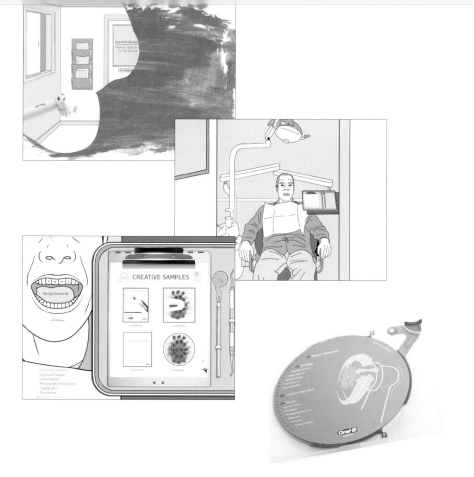

Corporate Image B2B
— CD-ROMs

agency
Arnold Worldwide/Boston
client
Oral B

Art Director:
John Weber
Writer:
Craig Johnson
Photographer/Illustrator:
Tim Kucynda
Programmer:
Steve Skroce
Digital Artist/Multimedia:
Casey Bearsch
Producer:
Jen Iwanicki
Designers:
Jim Badershall, Max Pfennighaus
Creative Directors:
Ron Lawner, Nick Kaldenbaugh,
Chris Bradley
ID:
04201N

Corporate Image B2B
— Other Digital Media

agency
Arc/London
client
Fiat

Art Directors:
Hilary Judd, Garry Munns
Writer:
Aaron Martin
Programmer:
David Greyling
Creative Directors:
Graham Mills, Jack Nolan
ID:
04247N

Corporate Image B2B
— Other Digital Media

Agency
Modem Media/Norwalk
Client
General Electric
Aircraft Engines

Art Directors:
Brian Waters, Himanshu Bharadwaj
Writer:
Stace Caseria
Agency Producer:
Burt Rosen
Producer:
Sarah Cravetz
Creative Director:
Joel Tretin
URL:
http://awards.modemmedia.com/
eno/04/oneshow/
ID:
04202N

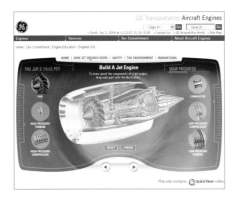

E-Commerce B2B
— Web Sites

Agency
IQ television group/Atlanta
Client
IBM

Art Director:
IQ television group
Writer:
IQ television group
Programmer:
IQ television group
Creative Director:
IQ television group
URL:
http://forwardview.showmail.tv/0401
ID:
04203N

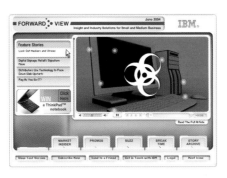

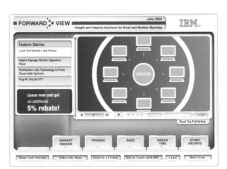

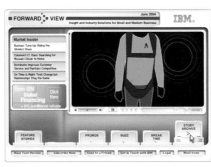

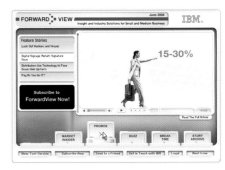

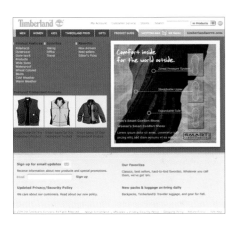

E-Commerce B2C
— Web Sites

agency
Fallon/Minneapolis
client
Timberland

Art Director:
Kevin Flatt
Writers:
Russ Stark, John Fox
Programmer:
Nate Hunsaker
Digital Artist/Multimedia:
Joel Herrmann
Producers:
Jonathan Maples, Michelle Domeyer,
Valerie Threatt
Designer:
Kevin Flatt
Information Architect:
Sam Spicer
Creative Director:
Kevin Flatt
URL:
http://awards.fallon.com/
index.aspx?camp=3
ID:
04204N

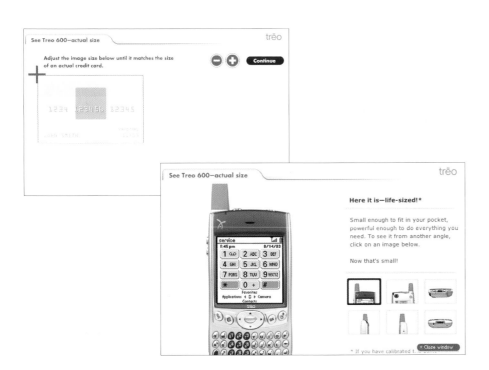

E-Commerce
— Other Digital Media

agency
Exemplum/Blacksburg
client
PalmOne

Programmer:
Exemplum Development Team
Designer:
Exemplum Design Team
URL:
http://www.exemplum.com/awards/
2003/oneshow/handspring/size/
ID:
04205N

Integrated Branding
— Campaign

AGENCY
Click Here/Dallas
CLIENT
Dr Pepper Raging Cow

Art Directors:
Brian Linder, Jim Kuenzer, J.J. Wampler
Writers:
Harley Jebens, Brian Linder, Jim Kuenzer,
Victoria Larroca, Matt Jones
Programmers:
Doug Knight, Yvonne Holmes,
Channing Womack
Digital Artist/Multimedia:
Shawn Scarsdale
Producers:
Michelle Wettreich, Jennifer Bryarly
Information Architect:
John Keehler
Directors:
Todd Copilevitz, Brandie Stepan,
Julie Sisemore, Erin Petty,
Kelli Powell, Jessica Vasquez
Creative Director:
Brian Nadurak
URL:
http://www.clickhere.com/virtualservers/
oneshow2004/drpepper.html
ID:
04249N

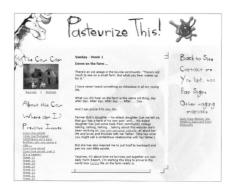

Integrated Branding
— Campaign

AGENCY
McKinney + Silver/Raleigh
CLIENT
Travelocity

Art Director:
Philip Marchington
Writers:
Lisa Shimotakahara, Bruce Fougere
Programmers:
John Magee, Max Newell,
Evan Lavidor, Howard Blazzard
Digital Artist/Multimedia:
Stacy Evans
Producers:
Cathy Wilson, Joann Brown
Designer:
Bruce Fougere
Information Architects:
Bruce Fougere, Jim Russell
Creative Director:
David Baldwin
ID:
04251N

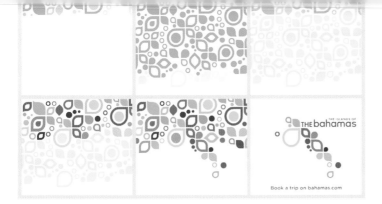

Integrated Branding — Campaign

Agency
Fallon/Minneapolis
client
The Islands of the Bahamas
Ministry of Tourism

Art Directors:
Tom Kunau, Nathan Hinz, Steve Driggs,
Tiger Porter, Dan Olson, Alan Leusink
Writers:
Russ Stark, Ryan Peck
Photographers/Illustrators:
David Bowman, Mark LaFavor, Various
Programmers:
Marty Davis, George Hilal, Nate Hunsaker,
Chris Stocksmith, Jim Park, Andy Lemay,
Jason Streigle
Digital Artists/Multimedia:
Charlie North, David MacDonald,
Joel Herrmann, Chris Stocksmith,
Ben Krueger, Aaron Padin
Agency Producers:
Christine Dennis, Jill Spitzfaden,
David Annis
Production Companies:
Hungry Man, Cosmo Street, Peep Show,
Sound Lounge, Framestore
Producers:
Laura Fischer, Julie Cammack,
Rob van de Weteringe buys,
Kate Hildebrant, Dave Lewis
Designers:
Nathan Hinz, David Mashburn,
Christian Erickson, Brad Surcey,
Dan Olson, Jeff Hale, Alan Leusink
Information Architects:
Marc Gowland, Sam Spicer, Mark Hines
Director:
John O'Hagan
Creative Directors:
Kevin Flatt, Joe Duffy, Todd Riddle,
Bruce Bildsten, John O'Hagan
ID:
04250N

Integrated Branding — Campaign

Agency
Ogilvy & Mather/London
client
Ford Sportka

Art Directors:
Rob Messeter, Mike Crowe
Writers:
Mike Crowe, Rob Messeter
Photographer/Illustrator:
Boris Vallejo
Producer:
Charlotte Lawrence
Creative Directors:
Malcolm Poynton, James Sinclair
URL:
http://www.creative-awards.co.uk/fordka
ID:
04252N

Integrated Branding — Campaign

Agency
OgilvyInteractive worldwide/
New York
client
IBM

Art Directors:
Cynthia Dauzier, Justin Gignac
Writers:
Jay Zasa, Jonathan Graham
Digital Artist/Multimedia:
Heavy
Production Company:
Pytka Productions
Producers:
Solange Claudio, Lee Weiss
Information Architect:
Paul Caron
Director:
Joe Pytka
Creative Directors:
Chris Wall, Jan Leth, Greg Kaplan,
Andy Berndt, John McNeil
ID:
04254N

Integrated Branding — Campaign

Agency
OgilvyInteractive worldwide/
New York
client
Sprite

Art Directors:
Alison Tsoi, David Korchin,
David Lloyd, Chris Curry
Writers:
Steven Nasi, Rob Rooney,
Brendan Gibbons
Programmer:
Josh Dreier
Digital Artists/Multimedia:
Scott Leisawitz, Drew Ziegler
Production Company:
House of Usher
Producers:
David Berenbroick, Lisa Steiman,
Stephanie Diaz Matos
Designer:
Slobodan Mileta
Information Architect:
John McGeehan
Director:
Kinka Usher
Creative Directors:
Chris Wall, David Apicella,
Jan Leth, Terry Finley
ID:
04255N

Integrated Branding — Campaign

agency
OgilvyOne worldwide/
London
client
IBM

Art Directors:
Howard Dean, Rod Broomfield
Writers:
David Shearer, Mark Davies
Programmers:
Fraser Campbell, Gary Jobe,
Thorkild Clausen, Peter Lewis-Dale,
Harsha Yogasundrum
Designer:
Zak Loney
Creative Director:
Colin Nimick
ID:
04253N

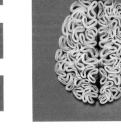

Integrated Branding — Campaign

agency
OgilvyOne worldwide/
Singapore
client
The Economist

Art Directors:
Richard Johnson, Dominic Goldman,
Kelly Dickinson, Naoki Ga, Craig Smith
Writers:
Richard Johnson, Peter Moss,
Dominic Goldman, Steve Hough,
Andy Greenaway
Photographers/Illustrators:
Roy Zhang, Kelly Dickinson, Procolor
Programmers:
Charles Yuen, Steve Lawler, Chandra Barathi
Producer:
Yow Pin Fern
Designers:
Dominic Goldman, Steve Lawler
Creative Directors:
Graham Kelly, Craig Smith,
Andy Greenaway, Dominic Goldman
ID:
04256N

Integrated Branding — Campaign

Agency
Periscope/Minneapolis
client
MasterCraft

Art Directors:
Andy Gugel, Doug Mickschl,
Mark Haumersen
Writers:
Katerina Martchouk, Kerry Casey
Photographers/Illustrators:
Kyle Johnson-MacPherson,
Florida Film & Video, Brad Fuller
Programmers:
Adam Knutson, Eric Hartmann,
Courtney Remes
Digital Artists/Multimedia:
Andy Gugel, Jesse Kaczmarek
Producers:
Klay DeVries, Marcene Hardy
Designer:
Andy Gugel
Creative Directors:
Chris Cortilet, Mark Haumersen
ID:
04257N

Integrated Branding — Campaign

Agency
Publicis/London
client
Hewlett-Packard

Art Directors:
Peter Hodgson, Robyn Garms
Writers:
Chris Aldhous, Martin Gent
Photographers/Illustrators:
MVOR, Katherine Brozenich,
Julian Abrams, Moose,
Erika Akerlund
Programmers:
Thomas Garrood,
Kaustar Bhattacharya
Agency Producers:
Vanessa Read, Suzanne Melia
Production Companies:
Ratpack Inc. at Annex Films,
Democracy, Krygier Hirschkorn
Producers:
Hans Elias, Fiona Campbell,
Nick Hirchkorn
Designer:
Douglas Mackenzie
Directors:
Kit Lynch-Robinson, Fred Lindner,
Iain Cadby
Creative Directors:
Jon Williams, Chris Aldhous,
Peter Hodgson
ID:
04258N

Integrated Branding
— Campaign

agency
TBWA\Chiat\Day\TEQUILA/
New York
client
Absolut

Art Directors:
Doug Jaeger, John Antoniello
Writer:
Ray Leggott
Programmer:
Ze Frank
Agency Producer:
Richard Coughlin
Creative Director:
Doug Jaeger
ID:
04259N

Integrated Branding
— Campaign

agency
Tribal DDB/Vancouver
client
Palmer Jarvis DDB

Art Directors:
Dean Lee, Alex Beim, Bruce Sinclair
Writers:
James Lee, Jessica Raya
Photographer:
CWS
Programmer:
Dana Brousseau
Digital Artist/Multimedia:
Jim Hebb
Producers:
Wendy Moriarty, Christi Rae
Designers:
Alex Beim, Dana Brousseau
Creative Directors:
Alan Russell, Bruce Sinclair
ID:
04260N

Brand Gaming
— Banners

Agency
ScreenPlay/Oslo
client
Norwegian Aviation College

Art Director:
Karl Petter Knutsen
Writers:
Andre Elvan, Karl Petter Knutsen
Programmer:
Andre Elvan
Producer:
Tone Bing
Designer:
Andre Elvan
Creative Director:
Karl Petter Knutsen
URL:
http://www.screenplay.no/one/nac
ID:
04206N

Brand Gaming
— Web Sites

Agency
Bascule/Tokyo
client
Sony Corporation

Art Director:
Shin Takeuchi
Photographer/Illustrator:
Shin Takeuchi
Programmer:
Shintaro Kanega
Digital Artist/Multimedia:
Shintaro Kanega
Production Company:
Bascule
Producer:
Ayako Abe
Designer:
Shin Takeuchi
Directors:
Hisaya Uike, Ken-ichiro Tanaka
Creative Director:
Mayumi Sato
URL:
http://cwa.bascule.co.jp/cwa.html
ID:
04215N

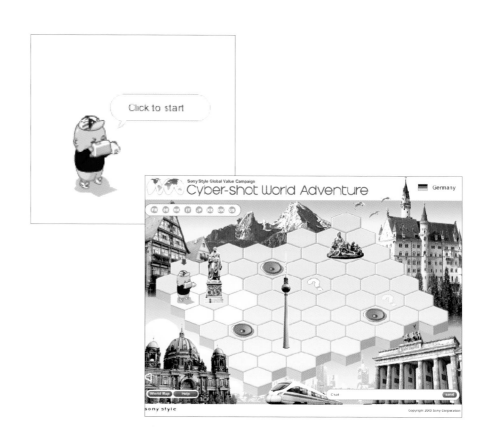

Brand Gaming
— Web Sites

agency
Bascule/Tokyo
client
Tanaka Garden

Art Director:
Mitsuhiro Oga
Writer:
Kampei Baba
Photographer/Illustrator:
Mitsuhiro Oga
Programmers:
Ken-ichiro Tanaka, Haruyuki Imai,
Kampei Baba
Digital Artist/Multimedia:
Yuji Nodera
Agency Producer:
Masayoshi Boku
Designer:
Mitsuhiro Oga
Creative Director:
Kampei Baba
URL:
http://faces.bascule.co.jp/ohayo/
ID:
04207N

Brand Gaming
— Web Sites

agency
deepblue networks/
Hamburg
client
Reemtsma
Cigarettenfabriken

Art Directors:
Stefan Grüner, Ninik Vogelsang
Writer:
Gerrit Dreher
Programmer:
Michael von Riegen
Digital Artists/Multimedia:
Stefan Grüner, Ninik Vogelsang
Director:
Ina Wagner
Creative Director:
Christian Thron
URL:
http://www.west.de/flowergarden/
oneshow
ID:
04208N

Brand Gaming
— Web Sites

Agency
Grupo W/Saltillo
Client
Bimbo

Art Director:
Miguel Calderon
Writer:
Ulises Valencia
Photographer/Illustrator:
Jezreel Gutierrez
Programmers:
Rodolfo Ruiz, Raul Uranga,
Homero Sousa
Digital Artist/Multimedia:
Ulises Valencia
Agency Producers:
Ulises Valencia, Miguel Calderon,
Marcela de la Cruz
Production Company:
Grupo W
Producer:
Ulises Valencia
Designers:
Roberto Espero, Sara Davila
Information Architect:
Miguel Calderon
Director:
Miguel Calderon
Creative Director:
Miguel Calderon
URL:
http://bimbo.grupow.com/juego
ID:
04209N

Brand Gaming
— Web Sites

Agency
Herraiz Soto & Co./
Barcelona
Client
Mahou

Art Director:
Andreu Colomer
Programmers:
Javier Alvarez, Xnografics
Creative Directors:
Angel Herraiz, Rafa Soto
URL:
http://www.herraizsoto.com/
festivales/juegomadridweb
ID:
04210N

 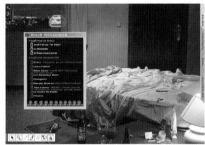

Brand Gaming
— Web Sites

agency
Herraiz Soto & Co./
Barcelona
client
Mahou

Art Director:
Andreu Colomer
Writer:
Paula Mourenza
Photographer/Illustrator:
Ricardo Miras
Programmer:
Javier Alvarez
Designer:
Andreu Colomer
Creative Directors:
Angel Herraiz, Rafa Soto
URL:
http://www.herraizsoto.com/
festivales/jfkweb
ID:
04211N

Brand Gaming
— Web Sites

agency
magneticNorth/
Manchester
client
Kellogg's Frosties

Writer:
Dave Bevan
Photographers/Illustrators:
Paul Neave, Catalyst Pictures
Programmers:
Paul Neave, Paul Barnes, Nik Lever
Production Company:
magneticNorth
Producers:
Janet Harrison, Jason Roche
Designer:
Paul Neave
Information Architect:
Jason Roche
Creative Director:
Brendan Dawes
URL:
http://www.kelloggs.co.uk/frosties
ID:
04212N

Brand Gaming
— Web Sites

agency
Pop & Co./New York
client
Cartoon Network

Art Director:
Jesse McGowan
Photographer/Illustrator:
Will Bredbeck
Programmer:
Karl Ackermann
Digital Artist/Multimedia:
Scott Gursky
Producers:
Kelly Galligan, Demetri Detsaridis
Designer:
Chris Koeppel
Creative Director:
Vincent Lacava
URL:
http://popandco.com/archive/
inuyasha
ID:
04213N

Brand Gaming
— Web Sites

agency
Ruder Finn Interactive/
New York
client
Ruder Finn Interactive

Art Director:
David Nicolaou
Programmer:
Erik Hansen
Digital Artist/Multimedia:
Kyung Jong Park
Producer:
Scott Schneider
Information Architect:
Neille Ilel
Creative Director:
Michael Schubert
URL:
http://www.mrpicassohead.com
ID:
04214N

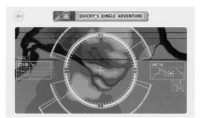

Brand Gaming
— Web Sites

Agency
Zentropy Partners/London
client
Nesquik

Art Director:
Andrew Tonkin
Writer:
Matt Hallet
Programmer:
Will Myers
Producer:
Tim Reeve
Creative Director:
Andrew Mason
URL:
http://www.nesquik.co.uk
ID:
04216N

Brand Gaming
— Web Sites

Agency
Zugara/Los Angeles
client
Sony Computer
Entertainment America

Programmers:
Patrik Karolak, Julie Han
Production Company:
Zugara
Producer:
Ingrid Moon
Designers:
Omar Puig, Patrik Karolak
URL:
http://socom2.playstation.com
ID:
04217N

Brand Gaming
— Other Digital Media

agency
Hakuhodo/Tokyo
client
World Wide Fund for
Nature Japan

Art Directors:
Takayoshi Kishimoto, Yuji Suzuki
Writers:
Toshiya Fukuda, Hiroko Ishii,
Michael Glenn
Photographer/Illustrator:
Yuji Suzuki
Programmer:
Yukio Sato
Agency Producer:
Shinji Fukao
Production Company:
TYO Interactive Design
Producers:
Kenji Morimoto, Yutaka Sugiyama
Designers:
Yuji Suzuki, Maki Sugihara
Information Architect:
Yukio Sato
Creative Director:
Toshiya Fukuda
URL:
http://www.tyo-id.co.jp/works/
banner/2003/wwf/04.html
ID:
04218N

Brand Gaming
— Other Digital Media

agency
Herraiz Soto & Co./
Barcelona
client
Jarabe de palo

Art Director:
Andreu Colomer
Photographer/Illustrator:
Una china en mi zapato
Creative Directors:
Angel Herraiz, Rafa Soto
URL:
http://www.herraizsoto.com/
festivales/jarabexmasweb
ID:
04219N

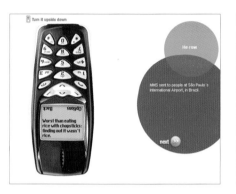

Wireless — Campaign

agency
Euro RSCG 4D/São Paulo
client
TIM

Art Directors:
Touche, Rodrigo Buim,
Fabio Matiazzi, Leandro Moraes
Writers:
Ana Dolabela, Fabio Pierro,
Cleide Oliveira
Programmer:
Hermas Junior
Producers:
Lucia Silveira, Valter Klug,
Carol Malinowski, Diorgenes Wenderly
Designers:
Lucia Silveira, Valter Klug,
Carol Malinowski, Diorgenes Wenderly
Creative Director:
Alon Sochaczewski
URL:
http://www.bluepuff.com/english/07/
ID:
04220N

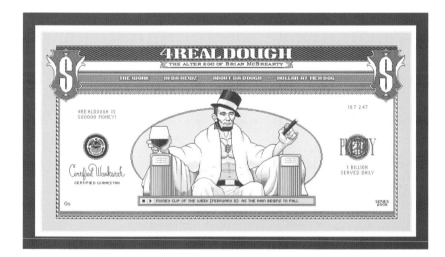

Self-Promotion
— Web Sites

agency
4RealDough/New York
client
Brian McBrearty

Art Director:
Trevor Van Meter
Programmers:
Luke Lutman, Jason Krogh
Digital Artist/Multimedia:
Trevor Van Meter
Designer:
Trevor Van Meter
Creative Directors:
Brian McBrearty, Trevor Van Meter
URL:
http://www.4realdough.com
ID:
04221N

Self-Promotion
— Web Sites

agency
AgênciaClick/São Paulo
client
AgênciaClick

Art Director:
Sergio Stefano
Writers:
PJ Pereira, Suzana Apelbaum, Veni Cury
Designers:
Diego Zambrano, Adhemas Batista,
Thiago Zanato, Fred Siqueira,
Douglas Alves, Thiago Cardoso,
Nara Maitre
Information Architect:
Alexandre Moreno
Creative Director:
PJ Pereira
URL:
http://awards.Agênciaclick.com.br/
404/en
ID:
04222N

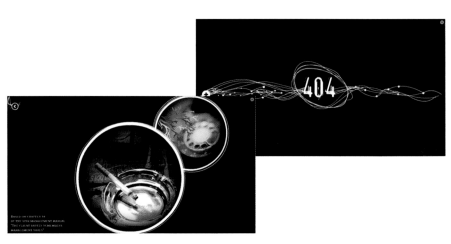

Self-Promotion
— Web Sites

agency
Arteaga Interactivo/
San Juan
client
Arteaga Interactivo

Art Director:
Ramón Reyes
Writer:
Odaly Santiago
Photographer/Illustrator:
Hector Ortiz
Programmers:
Ramón Reyes, David Sanchez
Designers:
Ramón Reyes, Hector Ortiz
Information Architects:
Ramón Reyes, Odaly Santiago
Creative Director:
Ramón Reyes
URL:
http://www.arteagainteractivo.com
ID:
04223N

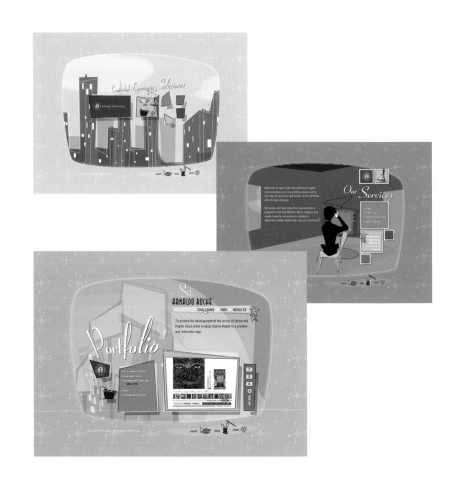

Self-Promotion
— Web Sites

agency
Eight x Ten/New York
client
Sean Kennedy
Santos Fotographie

Art Director:
Sean Kennedy Santos
Photographer/Illustrator:
Sean Kennedy Santos
Production Company:
Code and Theory
Producer:
Code and Theory
Designers:
Brandon Ralph, Dan Gardner
Creative Director:
Sean Kennedy Santos
URL:
http://www.Sksantos.com
ID:
04224N

Self-Promotion
— Web Sites

agency
Forsman & Bodenfors/
Gothenburg
client
Forsman & Bodenfors

Art Directors:
Mikko Timonen, Martin Cedergren,
Anders Eklind, Mathias Appelblad
Writers:
Filip Nilsson, Björn Engström,
Johan Olivero, Martin Ringqvist
Photographer/Illustrator:
Lennart Sjöberg
Programmers:
North Kingdom, Thomson,
Austronaut
Agency Producer:
Mathias Appelblad
Producer:
Mathias Appelblad
URL:
http://www.fb.se/eng
ID:
04225N

Self-Promotion
— Web Sites

Agency
Hamón-Associates/
Santa Monica
Client
Sharpe + Associates

Art Directors:
Scott Bremner, Kevin Hagen
Photographers:
Neal Brown, Comrade,
Hugh Kretschmer, Reimers + Hollar,
Jamey Stillings, Zachary Scott,
Eric Tucker
Programmers:
Jamandru Reynolds, Rory Ray,
Joe Mak
Producer:
Chandos Erwin
Designer:
Kevin Hagen
Information Architect:
Chandos Erwin
Creative Director:
Scott Bremner
URL:
sharpeonline.com
ID:
04230N

Self-Promotion
— Web Sites

Agency
magneticNorth/
Manchester
Client
magneticNorth

Art Director:
Suzie Webb
Writer:
Dave Bevan
Photographers/Illustrators:
Suzie Webb, Karina Lax
Programmers:
Adam Palmer, mN Team
Production Company:
magneticNorth
Producer:
mN Team
Designer:
Suzie Webb
Creative Director:
Brendan Dawes
URL:
http://www.magneticn.co.uk
ID:
04226N

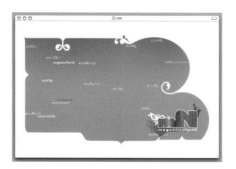

Self-Promotion
— Web Sites

Agency
Mother/London
Client
Mother

Art Directors:
Ben Mooge, Robert Saville,
Mark Waites
Writers:
Ben Mooge, Robert Saville,
Mark Waites
Agency Producer:
Emma Starzacker
Production Company:
Hungry Man
Producer:
Matt Buels
Director:
Mikko Lehtinen
Creative Directors:
Robert Saville, Mark Waites
ID:
04261N

Self-Promotion
— Web Sites

Agency
OgivlyOne worldwide/
New York
Client
Ogilvy North America

Art Director:
Tom Newsom
Photographers/Illustrators:
Jennifer Shedd, Jeffrey Bonacci
Digital Artist/Multimedia:
Tom Newsom
Producer:
Catherine Glover
Designer:
Nathalie Hennequin
Creative Directors:
David Israel, Brian Collins
URL:
http://www.wwpl.net/oneshow
2004/red/index.html
ID:
04227N

Self-Promotion
— Web Sites

Agency
Periscope/Minneapolis
Client
Periscope

Art Director:
Jesse Kaczmarek
Writer:
Kerry Casey
Programmers:
Adam Knutson, Eric Hartmann,
Courtney Remes, Todd Mitchell,
Jesse Kaczmarek
Digital Artist/Multimedia:
Jesse Kaczmarek
Producer:
Klay DeVries
Designer:
Jesse Kaczmarek
Creative Director:
Chris Cortilet
URL:
http://www.periscope.com
ID:
04228N

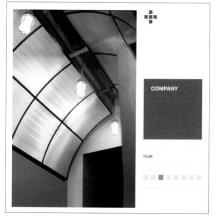

Self-Promotion
— Web Sites

Agency
SAY IT LOUD!/Orlando
Client
SAY IT LOUD!

Art Directors:
Julio Lima, Klaus Heesch,
Siege
Writers:
Julio Lima, Jane Harrison,
Tom Hope
Photographers/Illustrators:
Siege, Anthony DeLaura,
Caravaggio
Programmer:
Juicy Temples Creative
Digital Artist/Multimedia:
Juicy Temples Creative
Designers:
Juicy Temples Creative,
Julio Lima, Siege
Information Architect:
Juicy Temples Creative
Creative Directors:
Julio Lima, Klaus Heesch
URL:
http://www.sayitloud.us
ID:
04229N

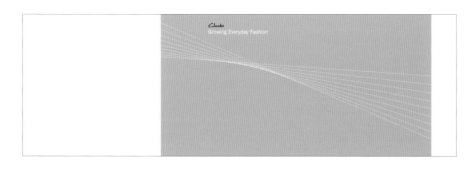

Self-Promotion
— Web Sites

agency
Taxi Studio/Abbots Leigh
client
Taxi Studio

Art Director:
Ryan Wills
Writer:
Spencer Buck
Programmer:
Chris White
Digital Artist/Multimedia:
Chris White
Designer:
Ryan Wills
Creative Director:
Spencer Buck
URL:
http://www.taxistudio.co.uk
ID:
04231N

Self-Promotion
— Web Sites

agency
Wonderlust Industries/
New York
client
Lyle Owerko

Art Director:
Lyle Owerko
Photographer/Illustrator:
Lyle Owerko
Programmer:
Tiberiu Craciun
Digital Artist/Multimedia:
Tiberiu Craciun
Production Company:
Evolution Studio
Producer:
Michael Costuros
Designer:
Michael Costuros
Creative Director:
Lyle Owerko
URL:
http://www.owerko.com
ID:
04232N

Self-Promotion
— CD-ROMs

agency
Matter/St.Paul
client
AdFed MN

Art Directors:
Andy Gugel, Jesse Kaczmarek,
T. Scott Major
Writer:
Erik Kválseth
Illustrator:
Jesse Kaczmarek
Programmer:
Andy Gugel
Producer:
Jolene Griffin
Designers:
Andy Gugel, Jesse Kaczmarek,
T. Scott Major
Creative Directors:
Andy Gugel, Jesse Kaczmarek,
T. Scott Major
ID:
04262N

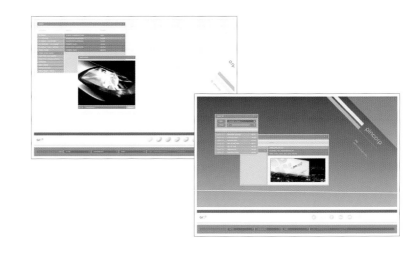

Self-Promotion
— CD-ROMs

agency
Periscope/Minneapolis
client
Echo Boys

Art Director:
Andy Gugel
Writer:
Sarah Branson
Programmer:
Bob Mueffelmann
Digital Artist/Multimedia:
Andy Gugel
Producer:
Matt Hattenberger
Designer:
Andy Gugel
Creative Director:
Chris Cortilet
ID:
04263N

Self-Promotion
— Other Digital Media

agency
Fort Franklin/Boston
client
Fort Franklin

Art Director:
Chris McRobbie Design & Illustration
Writer:
Marc Gallucci
Photographer/Illustrator:
Chris McRobbie Design & Illustration
Programmer:
Chris McRobbie Design & Illustration
Designer:
Chris McRobbie Design & Illustration
Creative Director:
Marc Gallucci
ID:
04264N

Self-Promotion
— Other Digital Media

agency
Mass/New York
client
Mass/Project

Writer:
Stephan Valter
Photographers/Illustrators:
Chen-Chieh Ni, Julia Koga Perger,
Stephan Valter
Digital Artist/Multimedia:
Stephan Valter
Production Company:
Mass
Designer:
Stephan Valter
Creative Director:
Stephan Valter
ID:
04265N

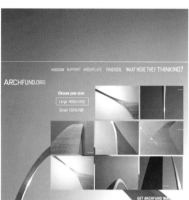

Non-Profit — Web Sites

agency
Arnold Worldwide/St. Louis
client
Jefferson National Parks
Association

Art Director:
Mark Halski
Writer:
Brad Fels
Photographers/Illustrators:
Mark Halski, Brad Fels
Digital Artists/Multimedia:
Taylor Dixson, Atomicdust
Designers:
Mike Spakowski, Atomicdust
Creative Director:
Mark Ray
URL:
http://www.archfund.org
ID:
04233N

Non-Profit — Web Sites

agency
The Barbarian Group/
Boston
client
Release1

Art Director:
The Barbarian Group
Writer:
The Barbarian Group
Programmer:
The Barbarian Group
Creative Director:
The Barbarian Group
URL:
http://www.release1.net
ID:
04242N

Non-Profit — Web Sites

AGENCY
BDDP & Fils/
Boulogne-Billancourt
CLIENT
Greenpeace

Art Director:
Robin de Lestrade
Writer:
Olivier Camensuli
Production Company:
BBD/Dans Le Sud
Producer:
Géraldine Fau
Director:
Ron Dyens
Creative Director:
Olivier Altmann
ID:
04234N

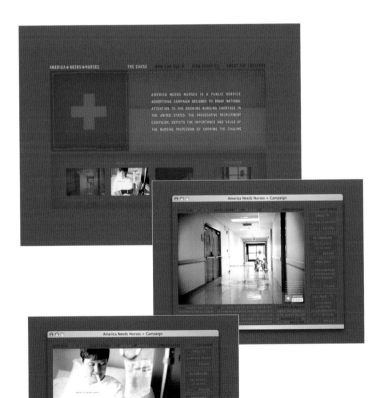

Non-Profit — Web Sites

AGENCY
BVK/Milwaukee
CLIENT
America Needs Nurses

Art Director:
Shawn Holpfer
Writer:
Gary Mueller
Photographer/Illustrator:
Bob Purman
Programmers:
Shawn Holpfer, Benjamin Gray
Creative Director:
Gary Mueller
URL:
http://www.americaneedsnurses.org
ID:
04235N

Non-Profit — Web Sites

agency
BVK/Milwaukee
client
Serve

Art Directors:
Shawn Holpfer, Brent Goral
Writer:
Gary Mueller
Programmer:
Benjamin Gray
Digital Artist/Multimedia:
Benjamin Gray
Creative Director:
Gary Mueller
URL:
http://www.servemarketing.com
ID:
04236N

Non-Profit — Web Sites

agency
Critical Mass/Calgary
client
NASA

Creative Director:
Critical Mass
URL:
http://www.criticalmass.com/
awards/oneclub_2004/nasa
ID:
04237N

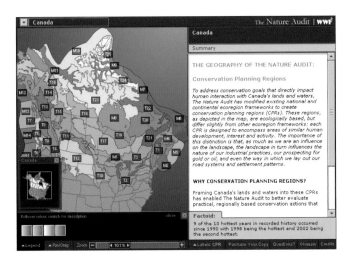

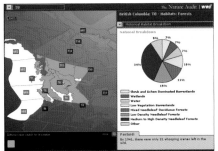

Non-Profit — Web Sites

AGENCY
epiculture/Toronto
client
WWF Canada

Writers:
Sheree Bond, Kevin Kavanagh,
Alexis Morgan, Lindsay Rodger
Programmers:
Matt Fabb, Cory Thomas
Digital Artist/Multimedia:
Don Yeung
Producers:
Te Thebeau, Lisa Horvat,
Ian Locke (WWF)
Designer:
Warren Davis
Creative Director:
Warren Davis
URL:
http://wwf.ca/AboutWWF/WhatWeDo/
TheNatureAudit/InteractiveMap/
ID:
04238N

Non-Profit — Web Sites

AGENCY
Euro RSCG Interaction/
London
client
Crusaid

Art Director:
Ross Elliott
Writer:
Alan Curson
Photographer/Illustrator:
Henrick Knudsen
Programmers:
Sean Chambers, Frazer Paul Harte,
Matthew Muller
Agency Producer:
Mario De Bortoli
Creative Director:
Scott Ex Rodgers
URL:
http://www.eurorscginteraction.co.
uk/awards/oneshow/cusaid/viral.htm
ID:
04239N

Non-Profit — Web Sites

agency
Periscope/Minneapolis
client
U.S. Marine Corps

Art Director:
Andy Gugel
Writer:
Katerina Martchouk
Programmers:
Andy Gugel, Adam Knutson
Digital Artist/Multimedia:
Andy Gugel
Producer:
Chris Cortilet
Designer:
Andy Gugel
Creative Director:
Chris Cortilet
URL:
http://interactive.periscope.com/
foreverhonor
ID:
04240N

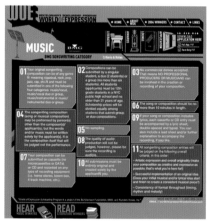

Non-Profit — Web Sites

agency
Platinum Design/New York
client
Bertelsmann's
Scholarship Program

Photographer/Illustrator:
Andrew Taray
Programmer:
Andrew Taray
Designer:
Andrew Taray
Creative Director:
Vickie Peslak
URL:
http://www.worldofexpression.org
ID:
04241N

Non-Profit — Web Sites

agency
Tribal DDB/Vancouver
client
Sea Turtle
Restoration Project

Art Director:
Bruce Sinclair
Writer:
Jennifer Hanson
Photographer/Illustrator:
Hurmoz Nabili
Programmer:
Dana Brousseau
Producer:
Monica Buck
Designers:
Dana Brousseau, Bruce Sinclair
Creative Director:
Bruce Sinclair
URL:
http://www.savetheleatherback.com
ID:
04243N

Non-Profit — Web Sites

agency
White Sheep/Helsinki
client
Nordic Institute for
Contemporary Art (NIFCA)

Art Director:
Markus Grannenfelt
Writer:
Tomas Träskman
Photographers/Illustrators:
Markus Grannenfelt, Niko Sipilä
Programmer:
Juha-Pekka Huikuri
Digital Artists/Multimedia:
Niko Sipilä, Mikko Karvonen
Producer:
Markus Grannenfelt
Designers:
Markus Grannenfelt, Niko Sipilä
Creative Director:
Markus Grannenfelt
URL:
http://www.grotto.tv
ID:
04244N

Non-Profit — CD-ROMs

agency
The Y&R Group/
Wunderman/Dearborn
client
Ford Credit

Art Directors:
Eric Livingston, Eric Eaman
Writer:
Jason Gitlin
Photographer/Illustrator:
Andy Suriano
Programmer:
The Furious
Digital Artist/Multimedia:
The Furious
Creative Directors:
Eric Livingston, Fred Stafford,
Doug Claggett
ID:
04267N

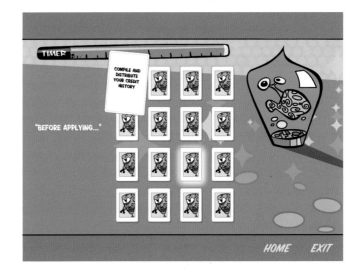

Non-Profit
— Other Digital Media

agency
Ogilvy & Mather RSTM/
Johannesburg
client
POWA

Art Director:
Ivan Pols
Writer:
Alison Hingle
Photographer/Illustrator:
Ivan Pols
Programmer:
Ivan Pols
Creative Director:
Gerry Human
URL:
http://www.wwpl.net/misc/
za_awards/powa_oneshow.html
ID:
04245N

Everyone ha|

Everyone has the right to dom of expr|

Everyone has the right to freedom|of expression with

amnesty international
WORKING TO PROTECT HUMAN RIGHTS WORLDWIDE

Non-Profit
— Other Digital Media

Agency
Saatchi & Saatchi AtPlay/
Cape Town
client
Amnesty International

Art Directors:
Gavin Cromhout, Uwe Gutschow,
Mark Mason
Writers:
Conn Bertish, Gavin Cromhout,
Uwe Gutschow
Programmer:
Gavin Cromhout
Agency Producer:
Uwe Gutschow
Production Company:
Lodestone
Producer:
Uwe Gutschow
Designer:
Gavin Cromhout
Creative Directors:
Gavin Cromhout, Uwe Gutschow
URL:
http://www.saatchiatplay.com/
awards/expression/
ID:
04246N

MAY 31 - WORLD NO TOBACCO DAY
世界无烟日 - 5月31日

Non-Profit
— Other Digital Media

Agency
TBWA\Shanghai
client
The Coalition for WNTD

Art Directors:
Eddie Wong, Leo Lee
Writers:
Eddie Wong, Jim Kuang
Photographer/Illustrator:
Leo Lee
Programmers:
Zhang Wen Yao,
Shanghai Real Star Technology
Designers:
Eddie Wong, Leo Lee
Creative Director:
Eddie Wong
ID:
04268N

Index